WORK BOOK

GOOD CHARTS

WORK
BOOK

SCOTT
BERINATO

GOOD CHARTS

Tips, Tools,
and Exercises
for Making
Better Data
Visualizations

HARVARD
BUSINESS
REVIEW
PRESS

ISBN: 978-1-63369-729-4
eISBN: 978-1-63369-730-0

The paper used in this publication meets the requirements of the American National Standard for Permanence of Paper for Publications and Documents in Libraries and Archives Z39.48-1992.

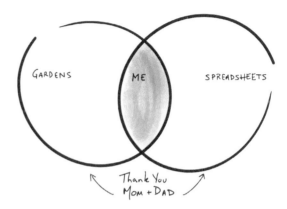

CONTENTS

INTRODUCTION

HOW DO I START?

HELLO.

You may have picked up this workbook after reading *Good Charts: The HBR Guide to Making Smarter, More Persuasive Data Visualizations*—my previous book, which offered a framework for understanding what makes good charts and laid out a process for creating them yourself. Or you may have picked it up in a shop just because dataviz intrigues you. You want to make good charts—or at least you think you should be able to. Maybe you got here through an online search. Or a colleague, a friend, or your boss handed you the book because he or she knows you like to think visually. In any case, you're here. And you probably have the same question most people ask once they decide that data visualization is something they want to learn about: *How do I start?*

When I speak or lead a workshop on data visualization, audiences are easily inspired by the transformations I show, and they understand the core argument of *Good Charts*—that what makes a good chart is not how pretty it is or how well it follows some set of chart-making rules but how effectively it conveys ideas by adapting to the context in which it will be used. But inspiration can be short-lived. Many feel overwhelmed by the idea of doing it themselves. So they ask me, *How do I start?*

Start here.

An analogy: For years I wanted to learn to play the guitar. I was inspired when I watched a friend play or heard a song with a deft guitar line. But I never picked one up, because I felt that same dread: I didn't know where or how to start. Finally, inspired by my daughter—who took up the guitar (and got good fast)—I decided to just start. With the help of a workbook, I learned notes, and then notes became chords. Eventually I added strumming patterns. Before long I could play a few simple songs, such as Bob Marley's "Three Little Birds" and Etta James's "I'd Rather Go Blind." I continued to build my skills and repertoire through practice, and although I'll never be a master of the instrument, I can work my way around it. In truth, it didn't take as long as I thought it would, and it wasn't as daunting to learn as I feared it would be. I just needed to start.

Good Charts Workbook provides the ideas and exercises to help you practice dataviz. They are its notes, chords, and strumming patterns—the foundational concepts and approaches that will soon have you playing simple songs. The workbook will help you understand *why* certain approaches to chart making work or don't work and prompt you to think through challenges yourself. It will allow you to test your ideas, and it provides a discussion about each challenge to help shape your thinking and build your dataviz literacy. It sets a foundation that will make the process of creating good charts as automatic for you as it now is for me to switch from a G chord to a D chord.

What do I need?

Let's keep this lo-fi. Most of the work that goes into making good charts does *not* happen digitally. Charts I create tend to be about 90% complete before I start digital manipulation. To get the most out of this workbook, you need:

Blank paper. You'll find blank work space here, right in the book. But extra paper will be helpful if you sketch the way I do—fast, messily, and over large areas. I don't like to feel constrained when I'm sketching, so spreading paper out over a table helps. Extra paper will also allow you to reuse challenges with others or to go back to them with fresh eyes after some time.

Colored pencils. I recommend having only a few of these available while you're sketching—say, a black one, a gray one, and two colors. (I use orange and blue quite often, but the choice doesn't matter.) It helps to make them contrasting colors so that you have the basic tools to show both complementary variables that can be different saturations of the same color and contrasting variables that shouldn't look as if they're part of the same group. I find that when a chart has too many colors, I focus more on refining its color scheme than on the expansive process of fast, idea-generating sketching. Once I get to prototyping, though, and I'm trying to create a viable, realistic, neat sketch of the chart, I like to add colors. With this workbook, you'll be both sketching and prototyping, so a set of about 10 colored pencils will serve you well.

Energy. Attacking these challenges when you're tired or not in the mood will be a slog. Sometimes my best ideas come after I put the work aside for a while and come back to it in a better frame of mind. Solutions that seemed elusive suddenly appear. Anyone who does crossword puzzles will recognize this phenomenon. The answer to a clue that irked you is suddenly obvious after you put it aside for a bit. It's the same with dataviz.

How is the workbook organized?

Two core sections make up the book.

Part 1. Build Skills

Each chapter in this part includes:

- A brief introduction to a dataviz skill, including six guiding principles
- A warm-up, including several small challenges to reinforce the guiding principles
- Three core challenges, each incorporating larger-scale tasks that address several or all the guiding principles

The challenges in Part 1 are organized according to the skills they're meant to develop. Their scope is limited in that they don't ask you to create something from nothing. In many cases the context (or multiple contexts) will be provided for you. The challenges are designed to focus your efforts on one skill at a time. You can flip to any challenge in the book—be it a warm-up or a core challenge—and try it, just as you could flip through a crossword book and pick any puzzle. Before you take on a challenge, though, it's helpful to read the chapter introduction and think about the guiding principles. Highlight key ideas from them. Everything flows from those principles, so it will be hard to get into the right mindset without having thought about them.

And although you don't have to tackle the challenges in order, the book does follow a loose logical progression, from more-fundamental skills (color, clarity) to more-complex ones (persuasion, conceptual charts). It's not a hard-and-fast pedagogy, but you may find it helpful to start at the beginning before jumping around.

Immediately following each warm-up section and each challenge, you'll find a discussion about it that includes my effort at solving it. I've deliberately avoided calling this an *answer key*. That's because I don't presume to have the *right* answer to any of these challenges. The charts you come up with could be completely different from mine and just as, or more, effective. In some cases I admit to being unsatisfied with my final approach or talk about the trade-offs I made to arrive at it. That's OK and entirely typical. It's rare that you don't have to make a trade-off to create a good chart. The discussions are not meant to tell you the answer; they're meant to expose my thinking to help guide yours.

Part 2: Make Good Charts

This part provides two large-scale challenges that require multiple skills from the previous section. They enlist the talk-sketch-prototype framework from *Good Charts* and are bigger and more open-ended than the previous challenges. I recommend that you save them until you've tried some of the skills-building challenges.

Just like the Build Skills section, discussions including my attempt at tackling them follow these big challenges.

In addition to these main sections, you will also find appendixes to help steer your efforts. *Good Charts Workbook* uses many chart types and reveals how the visual words and phrases you use to describe your data ("spread out," "a portion of," "distributed") may suggest a chart type for your given situation. To that end it includes some reference materials that show chart types, use cases for them, and some of the keywords associated with them. (These materials also appear in the original *Good Charts*.) They're excellent tools to have handy when you're in the process of talking and sketching. Wear out the back of this book looking at chart types and use cases and making notes about them.

How should I use the workbook?

First, I urge you to avoid short-circuiting the challenges—that is, don't read a challenge and then immediately flip to the discussion to see how I approached it. The workbook is meant above all to help you think for yourself about data visualization. Don't bias your approach by first looking at someone else's. No peeking! Hell, if it helps, tear out the discussions and put them elsewhere.

The skills-building challenges are focused and contained, but expand on them if you like. If you're working on a clarity exercise but see an opportunity to build some color skills, go for it. Want to create a new context for a challenge and then create a chart that reflects it? Go. In my discussions you'll see that ideas from multiple chapters pop up in any given challenge, because none of these skills can be completely isolated. Sometimes ideas about color find their way into a challenge about clarity. A persuasion challenge may require some clever choice of chart type. Use whatever you learn wherever you can.

Many of the discussions will include well-designed "final" charts, but you're not expected to create final products in this space. In most cases sketches and paper prototypes, or very neat sketches that approximate a final chart, are as far as you'll want to take your work. Get to a good idea and a good approach, and you'll have developed the material to create that final chart. As noted, most of the work that goes into making a good chart happens *before* you use digital tools to create the final product. Of course, if you want to work on your production and design skills as well, go for it.

On data and tools

On the charts and data in this book

Some of the charts in this book are obviously real. Others are based on real charts but have been changed substantially, whether in subject, data values, colors and labels, or any number of other elements. I've done that for several reasons—sometimes to protect proprietary data, other times to make the challenge more difficult or to change the context being addressed.

Several charts from *Harvard Business Review* and HBR.org are included here with the kind permission of Harvard Business Publishing. In some cases they have been reverse engineered to be poorer versions of what was ultimately published. That's for learning purposes only. The published versions are good charts; these rigged versions reflect neither the authors' nor HBR's intent.

Finally, some of the charts included here are simply bad: they suffer some fatal execution flaws or they're just a bit of a mess. Presenting something suboptimal gives you an opportunity to learn from and improve it. But it's important to note that while some of these charts are not ideal, they are *realistic*, in that they employ common approaches and techniques that I've seen in the world, online, and in my work helping others with their dataviz.

On tools

Next to *How do I start?* the most common question I hear is *What tools should I use?*

The answer is unsatisfyingly complex: No one tool works well enough to be *the* dataviz tool; many dozens exist, and more are coming online all the time. They all do some things well, and none of them does everything well. The more complete, more powerful tools—usually meant for data scientists—have a much steeper learning curve than those available free or for a small fee online.

I have about six to eight tools I use regularly, and I reevaluate every so often as new ones come online. I'm hopeful that soon we'll have good tools for non–data scientists that make the answer to this question much simpler. I've seen some tools in development that look extremely promising but are far off.

Search online once you know what kind of chart you're trying to make. Experiment with several tools and learn what you're comfortable with. Bookmark the ones you like. And remember, nothing beats a pencil and paper. You can get most of the way to a good chart with some talking and sketching.

I also advocate having another tool at your disposal: friends. If you know good data wranglers and good designers, or if your organization employs them, use them. I maintain a kitchen cabinet of friends and colleagues I rely on to help me with advanced data and design challenges. Dataviz is complex; it should be a team sport. More and more organizations are setting up teams to take on important visualization challenges. Put together a subject-matter expert, a data analyst, and a designer, and you'll up your dataviz game significantly.

One more thing you might find helpful is my workflow for creating (and re-creating) the charts in this book. Although I worked mostly on my own, I did lean on some people to help me, and you can imagine where in this process I'd bring them in.

1. I used an app called Sketches on an iPad Pro to take notes, sketch, and prototype. This was my "paper and pencil."
2. The data for this project was mostly stored in Excel or CSV (comma-separated values) files, where I created typical Excel visualizations just to have some initial view of the data.
3. I exported that data into an online tool called Plot.ly to re-create the initial Excel chart and manipulate it there. I also exported images from Plot.ly that I could import back into Sketches for marking up and discussing.
4. I used that same Plot.ly work space to create all the digital prototypes that came out of the sketch session. Those prototypes are generally not pictured here, because many are remarkably similar and wouldn't show enough progression to warrant the space they'd take up in the book. It's not uncommon for me to produce 10 to 12 very similar prototypes for a chart as I refine it.
5. When my digital prototypes felt close to complete, I exported SVG files from Plot.ly and imported them into Adobe Illustrator, where I have templates set up for my typography, colors, and other design standards. It's here that I polish my designs.

Let's share

Finally, I'd love to see what you create from these challenges and from using the talk-sketch-prototype method. To that end, I've created an email address (GoodChartsBook@gmail.com) where you can submit your charts—the befores, the afters, or both. Part of being a good chart maker is being a great chart user. Seeing others' work can be inspirational; sharing is a core ethic of the dataviz community. Even so, sometimes sharing leads to unwanted critique. The dataviz community can be oppressively judgy. That's not the goal here. I will not publicly critique anything you submit to me without your permission, ever.

———————

OK, you're ready. Wear this book out. Scribble notes all over it. Highlight things. Mark it up. Copy stuff. Take notes. Fill it with your ideas, your favorite approaches, color schemes you think are effective, and chart types you're particularly fond of. Critique my discussions. In short, use the workbook strategically, but really *use* it. You can always come back to it for inspiration or to look something up. I hope that when you're finished with it, this workbook is uniquely yours.

PART ONE

BUILD SKILLS

SKILLS

Now

5 chapters from now

CHAPTER I

CONTROLLING COLOR

"Some colors reconcile themselves to one another. Others just clash." —Edvard Munch

DMV NON-APPOINTMENT WAIT TIMES: SAN FRANCISCO VERSUS OAKLAND AREA

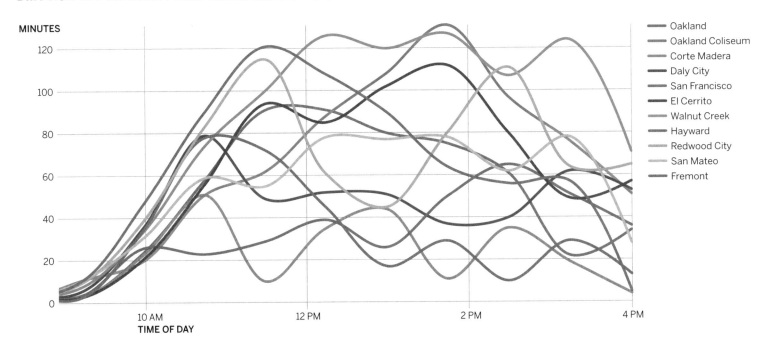

MINUTES

TIME OF DAY

Legend:
- Oakland
- Oakland Coliseum
- Corte Madera
- Daly City
- San Francisco
- El Cerrito
- Walnut Creek
- Hayward
- Redwood City
- San Mateo
- Fremont

IF YOU HAVE TIME to focus on improving only one thing in your charts, go after color. Most software can't intuit a good use of color for your context. It can't know how you want to group variables—which are primary and which are secondary, which are complementary and which are contrasting. Thus software tends to give every variable its own, somewhat randomly assigned color. Taken to an illogical extreme, your first output may be a mess of a rainbow like the above chart.

That's no good. Our eyes' ability to differentiate and remember colors flags after, say, five, or maybe seven. Most charts start with too much color. Your job is to identify the colors you need and then use only those.

You don't need to be a professional designer who knows color theory to make good charts with good colors. Just follow a few guidelines:

1 **Use less.** Stick to the minimum number of colors necessary to convey your idea. This is similar to reducing a fraction: sometimes we show $^{10}/_{15}$ when it could be expressed as $^2/_3$. Likewise, we may use eight colors when we need only four, or two. Look for ways to group items with the same color.

2 **Use gray.** Gray is your friend. It contrasts less with a white background, giving the sense of being "background information" behind the higher-contrast colors. It doesn't draw the eye the way stronger colors do. In many charts you can use gray for marks that the software automatically assigned a dominant color.

3 **Complement or contrast.** When variables are inherently similar, use similar or complementary colors. When they are in opposition, use contrasting colors. The audience will make the simple connection: Things that are alike go together; things that aren't don't. It sounds almost too obvious, but remember that the software doesn't understand this. If our eight variables all concern men and women of various ages, software will just assign eight distinct colors. I see an opportunity to use complementary colors for variables within each gender and contrasting colors between genders—say, four shades of green and four shades of orange. Two color families. Much cleaner.

4 **Stick to the variables.** Text, labels, and other marks that aren't part of the marks that are conveying the data information are best left black or gray (or white on a black background), with a few exceptions. Sometimes, connecting a label to line by matching the color will help, but be judicious. In general, using color for text decoration is distracting.

5 **Think how, not which.** Your impulse might be to think about *which* colors you want to use. But that's far less important than *how* you use color. Understanding background versus primary information, complementary and contrasting variables, and how to vary degrees of color saturation will lead to better decisions than just picking colors you like or your brand managers want you to use.

6 **Bonus pro tip: Consider the color-blind.** The power of a good chart can be lost if your audience includes people with various forms of color-vision deficiency—and it probably does. Up to 10% of men carry red-green color blindness, and 1% to 5% carry other forms. A color-blind person may see two colors as virtually the same. Good news: tools such as Coblis* and Color Oracle make it easier than ever to see how your charts will look to those with some form of color blindness. In my haste I often forget to check for color-blind-safe color schemes, but I'm trying to do better. Every chart in this book that wasn't deliberately designed poorly was checked for color-blind safety.

*See http://www.color-blindness.com/coblis-color-blindness-simulator/.

If you consider these guidelines, and understand your context, you can transform chromatic chaos into colorful coherence:

DMV NON-APPOINTMENT WAIT TIMES: TRY SAN FRANCISCO AT LUNCH, OAKLAND LATER

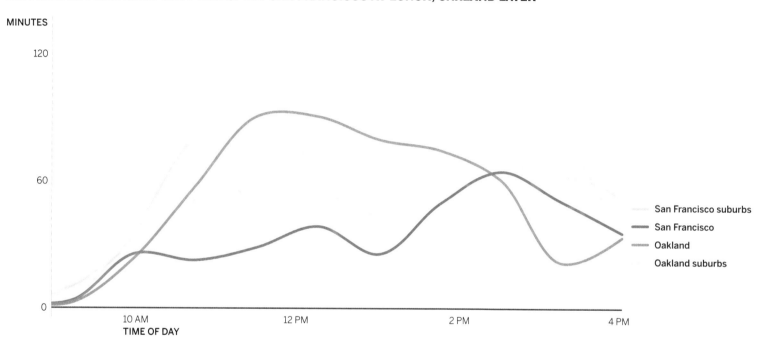

The following challenges are designed to help you develop color sense. Focus mostly on improving how you use color, following the prompts with each chart. For these challenges, don't worry about forms, and think about labels, value ranges, standard conventions, and other considerations only as they relate to the use of color.

CONTROLLING COLOR WARM-UP

1. In a bar chart, you want to show comparisons between older and younger men and between older and younger women. Which color scheme do you use?

    A — Men under 20
    — Men 20–40
    — Men 40–60
    — Men over 60

    — Women under 20
    — Women 20–40
    — Women 40–60
    — Women over 60

    B — Men under 40
    — Men over 40

    — Women under 40
    — Women over 40

    C — Men under 20
    — Men 20–40
    — Men 40–60
    — Men over 60

    Women under 20
    — Women 20–40
    — Women 40–60
    — Women over 60

2. In a scatter plot, you want to show the distribution of performance for four sales teams, but your goal is to highlight the performance of the European sales force against all others. Which color scheme do you use?

    A ● Europe
    ● North America
    ● Asia
    ● Africa

    B ● Europe
    ● North America
    ● Asia
    ● Africa

    C ● Europe
    ● North America
    ● Asia
    ● Africa

    D ● Europe
    ● North America
    ● Asia
    ● Africa

3. You want to compare before-noon sales to after-noon sales. Create a color scheme for the stacked bars.

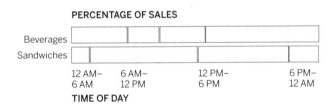

PERCENTAGE OF SALES

Beverages

Sandwiches

12 AM–   6 AM–   12 PM–   6 PM–
6 AM   12 PM   6 PM   12 AM

TIME OF DAY

4. You want to show answers from a Likert-type scale that ranges from "strongly agree" to "strongly disagree." Match each survey question below to the color scheme that would be best used to describe the results of that question.

   1. Please rate your feeling about the following statement: *I'm ready for the challenge of transforming this company.*
   2. Please rate your feeling about the following statement: *Our leaders are ready for the challenge of transforming this company.*
   3. Please rate your feeling about the following statement: *I believe in the company's strategy.*

A Strongly disagree   Strongly agree

B Strongly disagree   Strongly agree

C Strongly disagree   Strongly agree

5. In a line chart, you're comparing four price trends with an average trend. You want your audience to see the two lines that show below-average price trends. What's a good color to make the average trend line?

A A color similar to the ones used for the below-average trend lines, to show that they are what we want to compare with the average

B A color that contrasts with the below-average trend lines so that those two lines stand out

C Black so that it's neutral compared with the four trend lines

D Gray so that it's visible enough to use as a comparison but not dominant

6. In a chart about car makers, you have many variables. Group them to reduce the number of colors used and assign a color scheme. Find a grouping that requires only two colors.

AMC	FIAT	PLYMOUTH
AUDI	FORD	PONTIAC
BMW	HONDA	RENAULT
BUICK	MAZDA	SAAB
CADILLAC	MERCEDES	SUBARU
CHEVROLET	MERCURY	TRIUMPH
CHRYSLER	NISSAN	VOLKSWAGEN
CITROËN	OLDSMOBILE	VOLVO
DATSUN	OPEL	
DODGE	PEUGEOT	

7. Find four places to remove color from this plot.

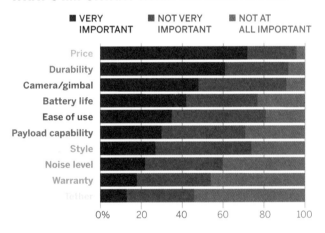

WHAT'S IMPORTANT WHEN BUYING A DRONE?

■ VERY IMPORTANT ■ NOT VERY IMPORTANT ■ NOT AT ALL IMPORTANT

Price
Durability
Camera/gimbal
Battery life
Ease of use
Payload capability
Style
Noise level
Warranty
Tether

0% 20 40 60 80 100

8. Create an alternative color scheme for the stacked bars above that will help the audience focus on important factors for buying a drone.

9. Find a logical way to reduce the amount of color in this stacked area graph.

12 COMMON MACHINE LEARNING TECHNIQUES

These approaches were identified through an analysis of more than 1,150 research papers over a four-year period.

PERCENTAGE OF TOTAL RESEARCH PAPERS

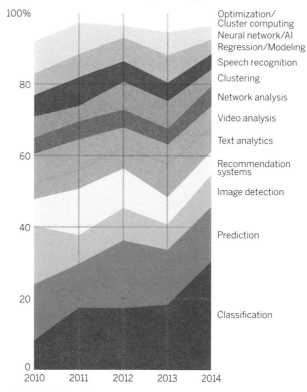

SOURCE: ACCENTURE INSTITUTE FOR HIGH PERFORMANCE, ANALYSIS OF A STANFORD MACHINE LEARNING RESEARCH PAPER DATABASE

10. What's wrong with this use of color, and how might you fix it?

WHAT'S YOUR FAVORITE COLOR?

DISCUSSION

Remember, what follows isn't always the right answer; it's just an answer. You may have come up with other ways to improve the use of color in these warm-ups, but these discussion points will reinforce good use of color in your charts.

1. Answer: B. The context focuses on a binary comparison—young versus old—so we shrink each gender into only two groups, under 40 and over 40. We give the two groups of men similar hues, and likewise for the women. Eight variables become four—fewer bars—and only two colors are in play. A obviously uses too much color, which would overwhelm the bar chart. The light-to-dark scheme of C maintains four distinctions per gender when we need only two. The gradient saturation also suggests different degrees of something. That could work for age, with younger people being less saturated, but it's not entirely intuitive.

2. Answer: C. Europe versus all others means we want the eye to go right to Europe. The other variables exist to be compared with Europe, and distinctions among them don't matter. Giving any other region a dominant color overemphasizes it, eliminating D (four distinct colors fighting for attention) and A (two distinct color groups, though the groupings don't mean much). B wouldn't be a bad choice, but making

three variables yellow would draw attention to that cluster, which would presumably have more marks on the page than Europe does, since it's three variables combined. By making the "other" group gray—and possibly not even labeling them separately but only as one variable called "other regions"—we leave no doubt: Look at Europe.

3. Simple, but we're following the context: We need to compare only before noon and after noon. The white hairlines between bar pieces enable us to see the subsections within the color groups. Other approaches that might work: lighter hues on the extremes to create a sense of "middle of the day" versus "early morning" and "late evening," or gray on the extremes, if "before noon" and "after noon" actually mean during waking hours only.

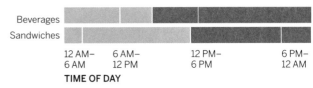

4. A: 3. If you want to show strong feelings in two directions, opposing colors on the extremes and lighter shades heading into the middle works well. Here lightness reflects ambivalence, and the hues reflect positive versus negative.

B: 1. If you want to show degrees of a positive feeling (readiness), try a desaturated-to-saturated scale using a single color. Here the darkness of the pink reflects respondents' degree of readiness.

C: 2. If you want to show degrees of a negative feeling (skepticism), simply flip the previous convention and move from saturated to desaturated. Here a darker blue reflects a deeper skepticism.

The distinction between answer B and answer C is subtle. No harm if you reversed your answers for those two.

5. Answer: C. Or possibly D. The below-average trend lines should get dominant colors, because that's where we want people to focus. At the same time, what matters is those lines' performance against average, so we don't want to overwhelm the average line. Gray might be too faint; a dark gray would probably work. If we chose A or B, we'd confuse the audience. In either case, it would appear to be another variable in the set, not an average line describing something about that set.

6. I created two groupings, one with three variables and one with two. Colors contrast in the grouping of three, since each represents a different region and I wanted to easily distinguish among them. The second grouping uses a dominant color and gray, because cars no longer in production are, in a sense, inactive (like the color gray).

- ● European
- ● American
- ● Asian
- ○ Cars in production
- ◐ Cars no longer in production

7. 1. *The headline.* Using color here doesn't help increase the focus on the crucial idea of what's important when buying a drone. Also, using the same color for the headline and the "not at all important" value seems confusing and contradictory.

2. *The category labels.* This rainbow is unnecessary decoration, and the colors don't connect to anything else in the visualization.

3. *The key.* Sometimes making the words in a key the same color as what they represent works. Here we're already using color blocks in the key. If we keep the blocks, the words can be black.

4. *The x-axis labels.* Associating these percentages with the variables' colors is confusing. After all, 80% of people would *not* vote "not at all important." In general, labels don't need color—especially color that's been assigned to something else.

8. Since the variables represent descending importance—that is, less and less of one thing—we can use less and less of one color to show that, making the least important group the least saturated. We still see all three groups, but we also quickly grasp decreasing importance in a way that's clearer than in the original.

WHAT'S IMPORTANT WHEN BUYING A DRONE?

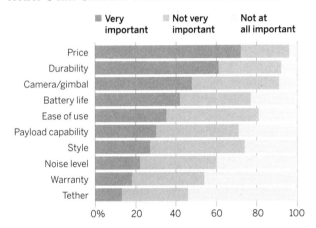

9. The stacked rainbow is fun to look at (I bet you saw it before you got to question 9), but it's extremely hard to use. Everything is fighting for attention. Any number of logical groupings could be created here: The top three categories as a group versus everything else—two colors. The top three categories each with its own color, and everything else as a fourth. The top half of the area as a group versus everything else in gray. Any of these would be a fine clustering, given the open-ended challenge. I chose to make three groups of four variables, with

the largest group getting a dominant color and the others getting less attention-grabbing gray and tan. This creates clear distinctions without overwhelming the eye, and it draws the eye to the large swath of most-common machine learning techniques.

12 COMMON MACHINE LEARNING TECHNIQUES

These approaches were identified through an analysis of more than 1,150 research papers over a four-year period.

PERCENTAGE OF TOTAL RESEARCH PAPERS

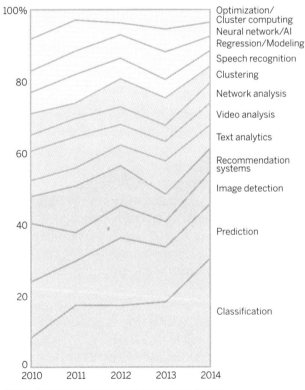

SOURCE: ACCENTURE INSTITUTE FOR HIGH PERFORMANCE, ANALYSIS OF A STANFORD MACHINE LEARNING RESEARCH PAPER DATABASE

10. While the simplicity of this chart is to be applauded, it looks like the first chart below to a red-green color-blind person. The easiest solution is to label the bars. But just to be sure, we can add cross-hatching to the two pieces to create a geometric distinction in case the colors are blending.

WHAT'S YOUR FAVORITE COLOR?

WHAT'S YOUR FAVORITE COLOR?

RED   GREEN

HOW WE SPEND OUR TIME

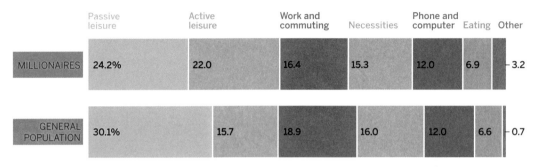

	Passive leisure	Active leisure	Work and commuting	Necessities	Phone and computer	Eating	Other
MILLIONAIRES	24.2%	22.0	16.4	15.3	12.0	6.9	3.2
GENERAL POPULATION	30.1%	15.7	18.9	16.0	12.0	6.6	0.7

THE RAINBOW BARS

Charts with many variables, each with its own dominant color, inevitably create a rainbow effect. Software will assign each variable its own color without regard for context. Rainbows are pretty, but in charts they're usually a detriment. Keeping track of what each color represents is difficult, and all the colors beg equally for attention. A second stacked bar with the same fruity palette makes this chart classic eye candy: captivating, but lacking "nutrition." It's hard to get meaning from it because it's hard to use. Let's work on it.

1. Find up to three places you can remove color regardless of context.
2. Find a way to group the variables using fewer colors but maintaining useful distinctions.
3. You want to discuss leisure time with your audience. Create a color scheme for this context.
4. Find a way to maintain seven colors without creating an overwhelming rainbow effect.

(sketch space)

DISCUSSION

Because the bars measure the same variables and are placed side by side, viewers assume that they're meant to make comparisons here. The best thing to do, then, is to restrict color to those places you want comparisons made.

1. The three places you can remove color regardless of context are the *headline*, the *bar labels* (Millionaires; General Population), and the *variable labels*.

   The data is colorful enough. Nothing is gained by adding color to the text. In fact, here it makes the headline fade into the visual. Giving the bar labels a background color is a design choice that adds confusion, not value. It makes the labels blend in, not stand out. They could almost be confused for another data category. Finally, matching the variable labels to their bars may seem like a good idea, but in a visual that already includes so much color, it's probably better to practice restraint.

   Here is the same chart with the color removed from those three places:

HOW WE SPEND OUR TIME

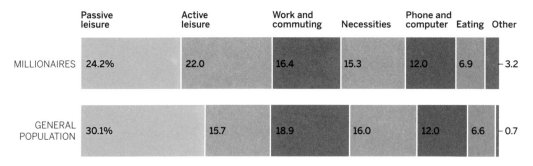

It's remarkable how much those three adjustments calm this chart down. It's still colorful, but it feels more manageable. Black on white, the highest contrast, makes the headline and labels pop. (Bonus non-color-related tip: Placing the labels between the bars would improve this even more, because they'd be adjacent to both visuals.)

2. To find a logical grouping, I had to consider how the variables are related. They fall into three groups: leisure, work, and survival, plus an "other" that I made gray, because "other" is often a small category of leftover data you don't want the audience to focus on. Which colors are used here is less important than making sure none of the categories use similar colors, because they're distinct. Making work and leisure two shades of red, for example, would suggest that they are alike in some way, whereas they're opposites. Finally, notice that "necessities" and "phone and computer" were swapped in order to group the variables. Because software automatically arranges charts according to how the data was entered, it's easy to forget this possibility. Remember that when sketching: just because the software does it a certain way doesn't mean you have to.

HOW WE SPEND OUR TIME

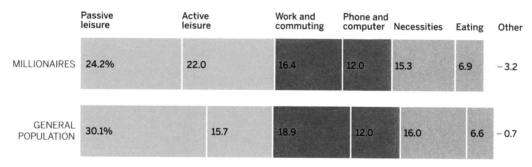

	Passive leisure	Active leisure	Work and commuting	Phone and computer	Necessities	Eating	Other
MILLIONAIRES	24.2%	22.0	16.4	12.0	15.3	6.9	— 3.2
GENERAL POPULATION	30.1%	15.7	18.9	12.0	16.0	6.6	— 0.7

3. In the crisp view on the following page, leisure is the focus so it gets color to draw the eye. Sometimes, to create focus, I'll make every variable gray and then start adding back color, variable by variable, until I feel I have enough to make my point. Here not only do we see leisure right away, but a natural dichotomy is created by removing color from the rest of the chart. Instead of seven variables, we see two: leisure and everything else. Additionally, since the top two activities are types of leisure, two

hues of the same color will show that they're complementary, not contrasting. Passive leisure gets a lighter hue because it feels softer (less active), but that's carrying the metaphor to an extreme. If it were darker but both forms of leisure were blue, that would be fine. Color coding the keyword in the label was a flourish; it's unnecessary, but in the absence of other color here, it doesn't fight for attention.

HOW WE SPEND OUR TIME

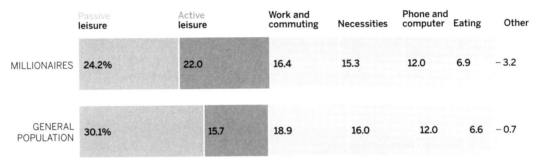

	Passive leisure	Active leisure	Work and commuting	Necessities	Phone and computer	Eating	Other
MILLIONAIRES	24.2%	22.0	16.4	15.3	12.0	6.9	− 3.2
GENERAL POPULATION	30.1%	15.7	18.9	16.0	12.0	6.6	− 0.7

4. This is a difficult challenge; I struggled to find a good solution. No matter how hard you try, giving seven colors equal billing risks creating that rainbow effect. To make each variable discrete but not overwhelming, I created white space and colored only the borders. I added color to the values and the labels to reinforce the connection. But I don't think it's terribly successful. For one thing, it adds emphasis to the numbers and labels and removes focus from the bars. If the numbers and labels are what I want you to see, why not just make a table? The value of the visual is diminished to the point of near uselessness. Am I comparing sizes or just reading the numbers? Also, some of these colors are difficult to read on a white background because of the low contrast.

I included this version to show that sometimes what you want to do isn't practicable. You must change course or make compromises. In this case, color manipulation alone probably can't maintain the distinction among the seven variables without overwhelming the eye with color. You need to attack something else, such as the form itself—and you will in later challenges.

HOW WE SPEND OUR TIME

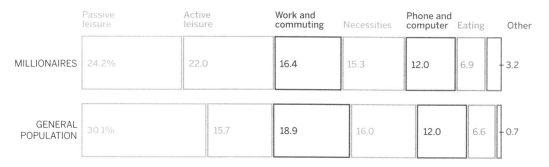

HOW INTERESTED ARE YOU IN BUYING A DRONE?

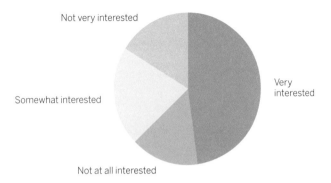

Not very interested

Very interested

Somewhat interested

Not at all interested

THE SIMPLE PIE

First, a word about pie charts. They are not evil. You will not be sent to charter's prison for making one. But pie charts are best for simple proportions with two to four pieces. They're most effective when one proportion is dominant—a half or three-quarters. More than a few wedges of more than a few colors creates a sameness among wedges that makes it hard to compare values. Because pies are simple, we often spend more time trying to design them up; after all, they don't have many pieces to manipulate, as compared with, say, a scatter plot. Here's an attempt at limiting color and the number of wedges in a pie that still doesn't hold up. Let's work on it.

1. Identify two problems with the colors used in this pie chart.
2. Remake the chart with a new color scheme.
3. You want your audience to see the proportion of people who have a positive interest in drones. Create a color scheme for this new goal.
4. You want to discuss only the interest in drones of respondents under 30. Remake the chart with a new color scheme to focus on that group, using the following data:

	UNDER 30	OVER 30
Very interested	34%	14%
Somewhat interested	14	7
Not very interested	5	11
Not at all interested	2	13

(sketch space)

DISCUSSION

The color scheme here, though easy on the eye, doesn't make much sense. It feels arbitrary. It doesn't highlight any particular grouping or idea. Sometimes color schemes like this result when marketing departments foist corporate colors on a presentation, or when someone tries to make an artificial association. If this were a chart about bananas, for example, the yellow might have been an attempt at cleverness. The best thing to do is to think about groups and use color based on that.

1. *The colors are not grouped logically.* I count two groups of variables: interest and lack of interest. But here darker yellows are assigned to "very interested" and "not very interested" and brighter yellows to "not at all interested" and "somewhat interested." Lightness and darkness aren't used logically.

   The colors do not proceed logically. Another way to think of the four variables is as a spectrum, from lots of interest to none. But the pie slices jump around that spectrum. If I assign numbers from 1 to 4 representing very interested to not at all interested, then reading clockwise (the way we usually look at pies) you see 1, 4, 2, 3.

2. Interested and not-interested groups are contrasting, so I use unlike colors. Within each group, though, the variables are complementary, so I use different shades of the same color, with richer hues for more-extreme feelings and less saturated ones for milder feelings within each group.

HOW INTERESTED ARE YOU IN BUYING A DRONE?

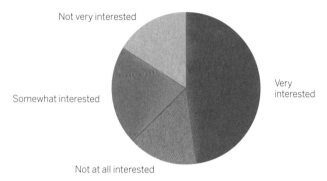

Now the problem with logical progression becomes immediately obvious. I want to compare interested with not interested, and that's difficult when those groups are broken up. So I rearrange the wedges:

HOW INTERESTED ARE YOU IN BUYING A DRONE?

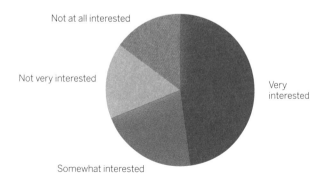

3. Removing information from your visualization can make a point more immediate, because it prevents viewers from focusing on the wrong information. Giving the not-interested group here a secondary gray and removing the labels signals to the audience to focus on interest in drones. One can intuit what the other wedges represent, but it doesn't matter; the idea is that two-thirds of people are interested.

HOW INTERESTED ARE YOU IN BUYING A DRONE?

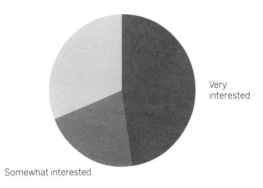

4. Initially you might try to do the simplest thing, which is to divvy up the pie with the demographic data. You don't want to introduce new colors or shades, because that will create eight distinct pieces and colors. The first attempt used simple dividing lines and labels. But although that allows us to see the under-30 interest in drones, it doesn't focus on that data. The user must go looking for it.

HOW INTERESTED ARE YOU IN BUYING A DRONE?

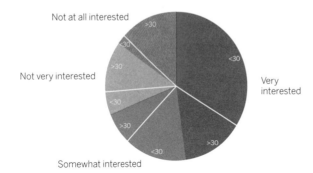

So again you can turn to gray to de-emphasize the over-30 respondents. That requires moving some of the wedges to make the under-30 pieces adjacent. The added subtitle ensures that viewers know who the focused wedges represent; without it, the colors would be confusing and the audience would wonder what the gray wedges represent.

HOW INTERESTED ARE YOU IN BUYING A DRONE?

RESPONDENTS UNDER 30

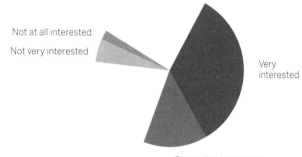

Not at all interested
Not very interested
Very interested
Somewhat interested

I'm fond of the way this chart puts the wedges in opposition, creating a real sense of *this* versus *that*. I quickly see the overwhelming interest.

What I don't see well is the proportion of all respondents who are under 30, because the gray wedges separate the under-30 data. (I have to mentally slide those green wedges to be adjacent to the pink ones, which is difficult to do.) I could change that if it were important in my context.

This is another fine approach if the total proportion of under-30 respondents is important. As a comparative tool, I still prefer the previous—but as always, context will dictate which to use.

HOW INTERESTED ARE YOU IN BUYING A DRONE?

RESPONDENTS UNDER 30

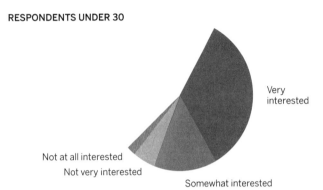

Very
interested

Not at all interested

Not very interested

Somewhat interested

HOUSE PRICE INDEX FOR SELECTED CITIES

Index: July 1998 = 100

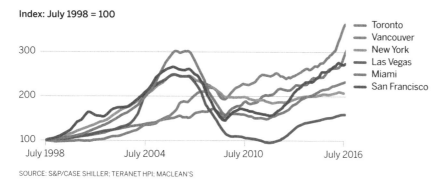

SOURCE: S&P/CASE SHILLER; TERANET HPI; MACLEAN'S

THE TANGLED LINES

Line charts present different challenges with color, because the variables converge, cross, and generally tangle together. Those color ganglia create a busyness that makes it hard to do what we want to do with trend lines: follow the trends. To test this, try to follow the San Francisco trend in the above chart. Let's work on it.

1. Create a logical grouping of variables and a color scheme for the grouping.
2. Create a color scheme that helps your audience focus on Canadian housing prices.
3. Create two more versions of this chart that use color to focus on trends in the data.

(sketch space)

DISCUSSION

The interaction of so many colors shifts our perception from six distinct trends to one general trend and then to the deviations from it, such as the two lines below the bubble. If we're meant to compare trend lines, it's nearly impossible here without some work. We need to find the trends we want people to see and think about foreground and background information and colors.

1. The most obvious (but not the only) grouping here is by country, which would reduce six colors to two. The difference in our ability to see the trend lines here compared with in the original is stark. We immediately notice those bold Canadian lines rising steadily past the U.S. cohort (and the changed headline reflects this). Notice, too, that the key has been eliminated and the labels are adjacent to their trend lines. This removes that small cluster of color in the corner, reducing eye travel. Now we don't have to dart between key and line to match colors to the cities they represent. I could have colored the city labels, but that feels extraneous here. If the lines were closer together, forcing the labels to be tightly packed together, color might have helped; but here there's plenty of space.

CANADIAN HOUSE PRICES RISE PAST U.S. PRICES

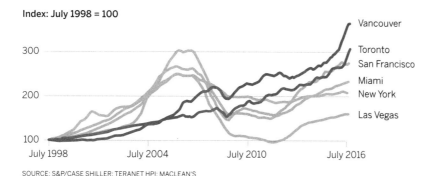

Index: July 1998 = 100

SOURCE: S&P/CASE SHILLER; TERANET HPI; MACLEAN'S

2. Could the pink-versus-blue chart satisfy this new context? Probably. But the blue does create an alternate point of focus. It's asking to be considered. Making the U.S. data the background context easily solves this: Background information becomes gray. The audience's eyes will go to the color. This time the labels are color coded, though I don't feel strongly about that. The most important idea is that we have one color to focus on. A green axis line at 300 calls attention to just how high Canadian prices have risen: above bubble prices! Your impulse might be to use a caption to do this—writing a sentence and using a pointer to explain what's going on. Usually a marker and good color use can achieve the same result. Overall, this chart has been rigged so that it's impossible for an audience to miss the point: It's time to talk about Canadian housing prices as a potential bubble.

CANADIAN HOUSE PRICES: STEADY GROWTH OR NEW BUBBLE?

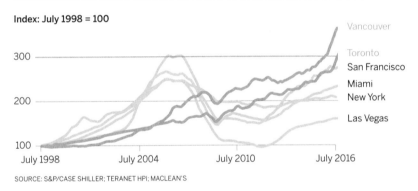

Index: July 1998 = 100

SOURCE: S&P/CASE SHILLER; TERANET HPI; MACLEAN'S

3. Even in this simple line chart, any number of trends can be highlighted. You could compare eastern to western cities, or coastal to landlocked, with two colors. You could highlight the most volatile and the least volatile markets. The two I chose to work on relate to the bubble.

First, I compared two cities that experienced similar bubbles but different recoveries. The humps match up, but a huge gap in value exists today. It's a comparison of different places, so I used different colors. I could make a case for removing the other cities altogether here. By keeping them, I've stumbled on an insight I didn't see before: Las Vegas is the real outlier, whereas San Francisco's growth commingles with that of other cities.

SIMILAR BUBBLES, DIFFERENT RECOVERIES

Index: July 1998 = 100

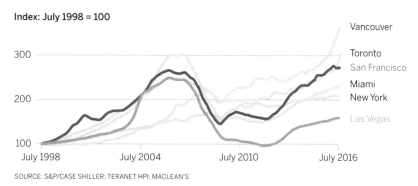

SOURCE: S&P/CASE SHILLER; TERANET HPI; MACLEAN'S

Second, I decided to use the same technique as in the Canada chart on the previous page to show that San Francisco prices are "bubbly" again. That simple color mark connecting 2016's level with the bubble makes the trend clear. Everything else is background information, downplayed with gray.

SAN FRANCISCO BUBBLES UP AGAIN

Index: July 1998 = 100

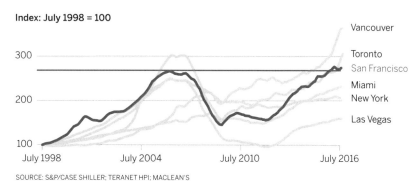

SOURCE: S&P/CASE SHILLER; TERANET HPI; MACLEAN'S

CHAPTER 2

CRAFTING FOR CLARITY

"For me the greatest beauty always lies in the greatest clarity." —Gotthold Ephraim Lessing

IF YOU FIND YOURSELF using text captions to explain parts of your visual, or if your audience asks you to explain how a chart is structured, or if—as happens to me sometimes—someone looks at your chart and blurts out, *What exactly am I looking at?* then the chart isn't clear. A clear chart communicates its ideas with little or no intervention. It stands on its own and sometimes produces what one data scientist (now an executive with the San Antonio Spurs) calls a "bliss point"—a moment when we feel we *get it*, instantly and without thinking.

That feeling is different from the one we get from eye candy—really pretty charts with gorgeous color schemes, curvy forms, and a multitude of data. Those are captivating but may or may not generate insight. Bliss points produce a flash of instant understanding. They don't even have to be pretty. Compare:

Eye candy:

SNAKE BITES IN AUSTRALIA

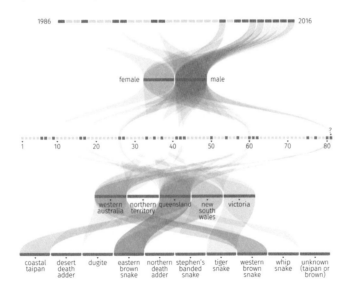

BY MATT GOULD, CC BY-SA 4.0, HTTPS://COMMONS.WIKIMEDIA.ORG/W/INDEX.PHP?CURID=58876507.

Bliss point:

POLIO

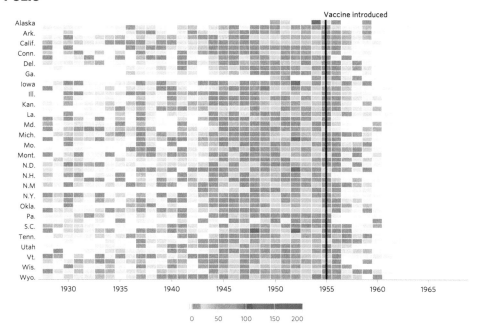

REPUBLISHED WITH PERMISSION OF DOW JONES INC., FROM WSJ.COM, "BATTLING INFECTIOUS DISEASES IN THE 20TH CENTURY: THE IMPACT OF VACCINES" BY TYNAN DEBOLD AND DOV FRIEDMAN; PERMISSION CONVEYED THROUGH COPYRIGHT CLEARANCE CENTER, INC.

The first chart is gorgeous but takes work to figure out. It's unclear how the twisting bands function beyond grabbing our attention. They make it harder to get to the meaning. The idea in the second chart hits us almost as soon as we see it. That's what you're aiming for.

Sometimes simplicity helps achieve clarity, but simple things aren't always clear, and clear things don't have to be simple. To achieve clarity, to get to those bliss points, requires more than nice colors and sparse, simple designs. Every mark on a chart that requires the audience to stop and consider, to make decisions about where to focus, to challenge how they normally think, works against clarity. Use these guidelines to achieve a clear design.

1 **Take stuff away.** Think about every mark on your chart and ask, *Is this necessary to make my point?* Often extraneous axis labels and distracting grid lines, for example, which are generated automatically by chart-making programs, get left in. Unnecessary color can pull attention away from the core idea. Be aggressive. Even try to delete variables altogether if you think you can make your point without them.

2 **Remove redundancy.** A headline that reads "Sales vs. Revenue" just repeats the axis labels. Captions that simply describe what the visual shows add no insight. Axes representing dollars or percentages don't need $ or % repeated on every label. Look for places in your dataviz where information is repeated and take as much as you can off the page while maintaining clarity.

3 **Limit color and eye travel.** Color is powerful—and distracting. If eye-catching colors are assigned to noncore elements, they'll fight for attention. Think of color as a fraction that needs to be reduced. You want to show $\frac{2}{3}$, not $\frac{12}{18}$. Do this by grouping variables and using gray for contextual, secondary information. Keys, legends, and captions with pointers force eye travel. It may seem trivial to have to look to the right corner for the key and then back to the visual, repeating the process three or four times, but it's not. Darting back and forth, or following long lines to labels, slows down chart reading significantly. The farther the information is from what it references, the longer the trek for the eyes. Keep labels and captions close to the parts of the visual they reference. In line charts I like to put labels at the ends of the lines they represent; they make a natural stopping point for eyes scanning the visual, and they remove the need for a key.

4 **Know how people think.** The brain works on heuristics. It takes shortcuts. In our minds, the future always comes *after* the present—to the right of it. Values go *up*, with higher values *above* lower ones. In general red means *hot* or *danger* or *bad*, while blue is *cool* or *water*, and green is *good* or *safe*. When you design *against* such neurological conventions, viewers must work hard to get past it. Imagine trying to read a timeline from right to left, or a y-axis with 0 at the top and 100% at the bottom. Respect convention—and take

advantage of it. If a trend is worrisome, make it red. Put a higher value literally higher than others on your chart. Put North up and South down.

5 **Describe ideas, not structure.** Use text, headlines, captions, and other visual markers to highlight ideas or insights rather than to describe the visualization's architecture. Headlines that reiterate the form don't help the audience as much as ones that hint at or explicitly state why the visual exists. Compare, for example, "Distribution of Spending on Health Care and Wellness" with "More Spending Doesn't Increase Wellness." Or "Trend Line of Median Operating Losses by Year" with "Losses Are Mounting."

6 **Bonus pro tip: Align everything.** This simple guideline is supremely effective at creating visual order. The sense of clutter and murkiness that some charts produce comes in part from the way items float independently throughout the visual space. Axis labels are centered on their axes and tilted. Captions hover wherever there happens to be white space. Use the y-axis as a left alignment, establish a second point with which to align captions and other labels, and the cluttered feeling will disappear.

Clarity isn't easy, and it takes courage. Chart makers tend to stuff everything they have into their visuals—variables, labels, colors. Maybe they're not sure what the central idea is; maybe they want all the data there to show the boss how busy they are. It may be comforting to the chart makers, but it makes their visualizations inaccessible or, worse, impenetrable for users. Presenting a clear chart that says one thing well may discomfit you at first, but your audience will appreciate it.

The following challenges are intended to improve clarity. Focus mostly on ways to remove confusion and clutter, using the prompts with each chart. Don't worry about forms, and think about color, labels, standard conventions, and other considerations only as they relate to creating clarity.

CRAFTING FOR CLARITY WARM-UP

1. You want to use a line chart to show the year-to-year trend in three forecasts. Which grid creates the clearest experience for that context?

A FORECAST

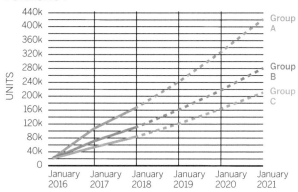

B FORECAST

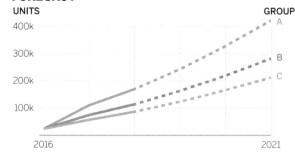

C FORECAST

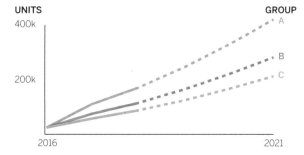

2. Find a common element in the following bar charts that makes both unclear. Find one element in each that makes it uniquely unclear.

MEASURING THE DISTANCE AND BRIGHTNESS OF NEARBY GALAXIES

Distance in parsecs is shown on the left side, and brightness in apparent magnitude is shown on the right.

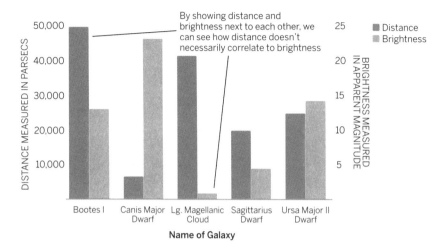

By showing distance and brightness next to each other, we can see how distance doesn't necessarily correlate to brightness

DISTANCE AND BRIGHTNESS

They vary by galaxy.

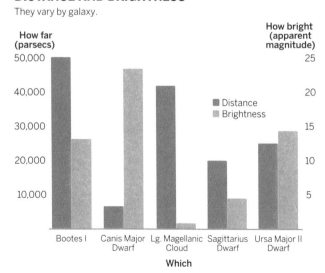

3. True or false: To make a chart clearer, you should always remove as many things from the visualization as you can.

4. Will a data visualization plotted on these axes be clear? Why?

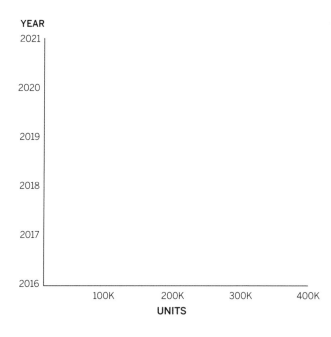

5. In a scatter plot you want to plot average health care spending against average life expectancy for several countries. The plot will show a positive correlation across all countries except one: the United States, which spends the most but achieves only a middle-to-low life expectancy. Which headline would you choose for clarity?

A   Health Care Spending vs. Life Expectancy for Several Countries
B   Investing in Health Care Works—Nearly Everywhere
C   Countries That Spend More on Health Care Live Longer
D   What Does Health Care Spending Tell Us About Life Expectancy?

6. What makes this pie chart less clear than it could be? How would you fix it?

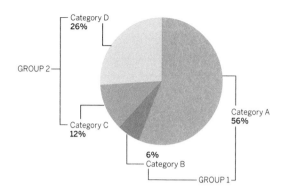

7. You want to show customers' relative happiness or anger by region on a map. Which color scheme will be clearest?

8. Without knowing what this scatter plot is about, what in the visual field would you attack first to improve its clarity?

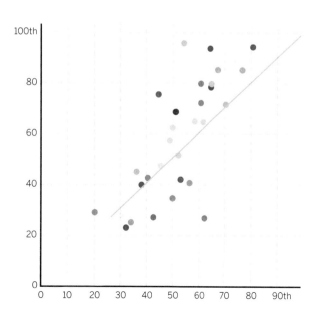

9. Here is an expansion of the same scatter plot made less clear by the number of alignment points. Mark all the horizontal and vertical alignment points.

10. After improving the chart's alignment, find other ways to make it clearer and sketch a new version.

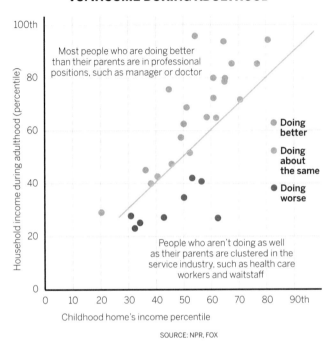

HOUSEHOLD INCOME DURING CHILDHOOD VS. INCOME DURING ADULTHOOD

Household income during adulthood (percentile)

Most people who are doing better than their parents are in professional positions, such as manager or doctor

Doing better

Doing about the same

Doing worse

People who aren't doing as well as their parents are clustered in the service industry, such as health care workers and waitstaff

Childhood home's income percentile

SOURCE: NPR, FOX

DISCUSSION

1. Answer: B. The key is the context of needing to talk about "year-to-year trends." That disqualifies C, which—in an effort to be as simple as possible—has literally removed any sign of those trends. In a presentation in which the five-year trend matters, it might be a fine chart, but it's not enough for our context. The first chart, A, also provides year-to-year trends, but it's probably not simple enough. The number and heaviness of the grid lines on the y-axis make it hard to read. If those grid lines were lighter, as in B, one could argue that they're useful. They give us more-exact values at each year's intersecting grid line. But even if the lines weren't so dominant, it would be hard to connect them to their value, because values are scrunched together. You could make the chart higher to create more space between values, but even then the visual busyness would fight the trend lines.

   Notice some other small adjustments between A and B that make B clearer: Labels have been aligned. The word "group" is used once rather than repeated in three colors. The redundant "January" on the x-axis labels has been removed because it wasn't helpful.

2. *Common element:* The categories on the x-axis are organized alphabetically. Although that's a valid way to organize information, it's not clarifying here—it just creates a haphazard collection of comparisons. And galaxies are not arranged alphabetically in the universe. We're comparing distances and brightness. Arranging the galaxies on one of those progressions—nearest to farthest, or brightest to dimmest—would provide an anchor point for seeing what one variable does to the other. To me, distance is the more accessible variable, so I would arrange the data to progress from near to far. Far to near would challenge a perceptual convention that we start on the left with the nearest thing. It would feel weird to start with the farthest away and progress to the nearest.

   Unique unclear element: For chart 1, it's redundancy. The chart is laden with repetition. The title, the subtitle, both y-axes, the key, and the caption all effectively say the same thing. If you identified the pointers, that's also a good catch. It's confusing to have the pointers refer to bars from different galaxies, and the long lines create visual distraction, too.

   For chart 2, it's ambiguity. This chart fixes many of the previous version's problems, but it oversimplifies. The title is vague—distance and brightness of what?—and the subtitle is reflexively obvious. It doesn't help us understand why we're looking at this thing. The axis labels are nice and short, but what do they refer to? How far is what? How bright is what? The label

"Which" on the x-axis is aggressively unclear. If you don't know that Bootes I et al. are galaxies, you're lost. But even if we imagine that we can figure out this presentation, the arrangement of the data will thwart us. I find myself asking, *What does this mean?* It looks more like a thoughtless display of data than a visual that conveys an idea. What's the point?

Here's a reimagined attempt to create clarity through a balance of simplicity and well-organized information. Notice that variables are arranged by increasing distance, which highlights the idea that brightness doesn't follow an inverse pattern. I reinforced that with the headline and then cleaned up the axis labels and created fewer points of alignment.

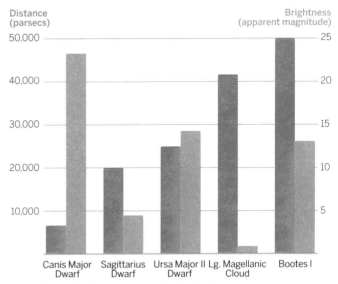

FARAWAY GALAXIES SHINE BRIGHT, OTHERS ARE DIM

Distance (parsecs) — Brightness (apparent magnitude)

Name of galaxy from nearest to farthest

3. Answer: False. Simplicity is valuable, but only to a point. Take away too much, and you're left with ambiguity. A chart that's too simple is as unclear as a cluttered mess. Einstein is credited with saying, "Everything should be made as simple as possible, but not simpler." Don't simplify so much that you can't still quickly grasp the core ideas in the visual. Complex things can be clear if they're thoughtfully organized.

4. *It will be unclear.* The axes are transposed in a way that feels unnatural. Time going up the y-axis doesn't make much sense, because we think of time as going left to right. Flouting that kind of expectation creates needless difficulty for the audience. To see just how neurologically disruptive this is, look at this plot on those axes and try to answer simple questions such as *Which group is growing the most? In what year does Group B cross 200,000 units?* You're probably tilting your head to make the y-axis seem like the x-axis. But if you do that, you'll see an x-axis that goes backward, right to left. It all makes for a terribly unclear experience.

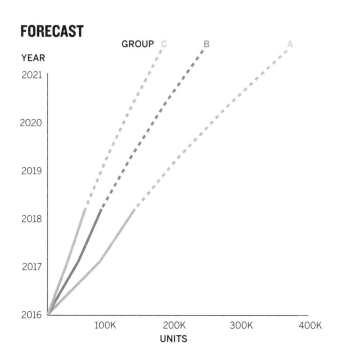

FORECAST

5. Answer: B. This title comes closest to conveying the idea we want people to see: The United States is an outlier. The others would not be wrong, but each suffers from some short-coming. C comes close to revealing the idea, but it doesn't acknowledge the outlier—which is the focus not only for us but also for anyone who looks at the chart. Outliers draw the eye. This headline also contains a grammatical gaffe: countries don't live longer; people in countries do.

    More obviously unclear, A simply describes the axes and the variables. It says what other parts of the visual show, and it doesn't do enough work. D is tempting because it invites people looking at the chart to answer the question with what they see—which, again, will be the outlier. What does it tell us? That the United States is different, and not in a good way. It feels just a bit too open-ended in this case, though question titles can be effective when the answer in the visual is blatantly clear. (In fact, as I look at it, I have a hard time thinking D is "wrong" here, though I'd still use B.)

6. The lines make this chart much less clear than it could be. For one thing, they create too much eye travel. Connecting the visual element to its label requires some navigation, and it's not direct navigation. It's work to follow all the elbows in those pointers. Also, nothing is aligned and labels are placed at different and arbitrary distances from the chart. The Group

labels are the most puzzling choice here: they create extra lines, they're far from the visual, and they're redundant. We've already created groups with color. There's no need to label them again.

7. Answer: A. On this spectrum we want colors to fit convention. Because we associate red with heat and negativity, it makes sense to increase red's intensity as the anger level rises. This is especially true when the juxtaposed color is green, which is associated with safety and positivity. Those conventions make C a poor choice. Regions colored in deep red on a map would not immediately convey "happy customers." As for the gray scale of B, it's not bad, but it's linear. Instead of conveying a comparison of happy versus sad, it suggests a degree of one variable: anger.

8. *Color.* Try to imagine the key for this chart, with more than two dozen. The alternative to a key would be labeling each dot—which would create a rough sea of labels tossed about in the visual space. The best way to attack color here is to find logical groupings of the variables that significantly reduce the number of colors.

9. Marking the alignments in a chart is a good exercise for identifying visual clutter and eliminating it. Make sure you find both horizontal and vertical points of alignment for various elements. Here I've found 10 points of alignment. That's too many. Notice, too, how the captions float between grid lines—which are natural places to align material. The chart already has two axes that can be used for alignment, and as you add elements, you want to align as many as possible on as few alignment points as possible.

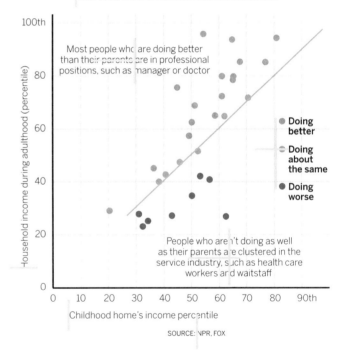

HOUSEHOLD INCOME DURING CHILDHOOD VS. INCOME DURING ADULTHOOD

Most people who are doing better than their parents are in professional positions, such as manager or doctor

Doing better

Doing about the same

Doing worse

People who aren't doing as well as their parents are clustered in the service industry, such as health care workers and waitstaff

Household income during adulthood (percentile)

Childhood home's income percentile

SOURCE: NPR, FOX

10. I'm not thrilled by those pointers from the captions—they're long, and they cross the linear slope line that shows a statistical fit for the data, creating a bit of traffic—but I made the trade-off of including them because I thought a key and captions would have been even more disruptive. Still, as I look at it now, the color in the caption may be enough to make the connection. I may not need the pointers after all. To offset the use of pointers, I removed some of the x-axis grid lines. The captions do double duty here, helping to explain the idea and serving as a key. Using color for the words that would have been repeated in a key saves an element. Everything else is aligned left. This version shows the power of alignment: I've added a caption and three pointers, yet it feels much clearer.

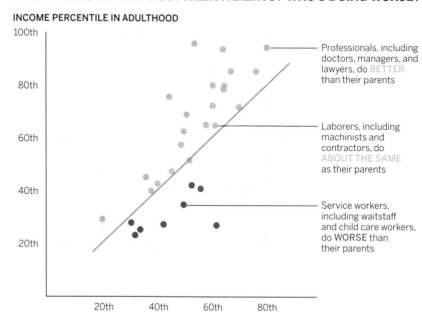

WHO'S DOING BETTER THAN THEIR PARENTS? WHO'S DOING WORSE?

INCOME PERCENTILE IN ADULTHOOD

Professionals, including doctors, managers, and lawyers, do BETTER than their parents

Laborers, including machinists and contractors, do ABOUT THE SAME as their parents

Service workers, including waitstaff and child care workers, do WORSE than their parents

PARENTS' INCOME DURING CHILDHOOD

SOURCE: NPR, VOX

HOUSE PRICES AND INCOME AROUND THE WORLD

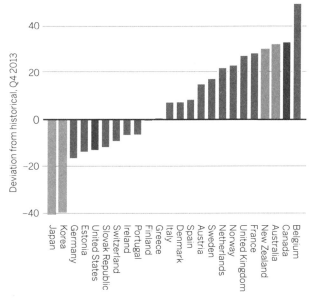

SOURCE: OECD AND IMF CALCULATIONS

THE SIMPLE, UNCLEAR BAR CHART

It's tempting to think that a chart with ample white space, few words, and a clean design will be clear, but it might not be. In general, simplicity leads to clarity, but sometimes less is less. Simplicity fails when we're forced to stop and think about what we're looking at. If the audience is asking for information that's not there, the chart is probably too simple. Missing or confusing labels, visual elements that draw the eye without explanation, and clever but obtuse headlines are some of the ways simplicity can go awry, as it has here. Let's work on it.

1. Identify four elements of this chart that contribute to a lack of clarity.
2. Sketch a new version of it given the following contextual information:

   a. The y-axis shows a percentage deviation from the historical average ratio of house price to income during the fourth quarter of 2013.
   b. Large positive deviations from historical averages may signal a housing bubble.

(sketch space)

DISCUSSION

This is obscurity disguised as simplicity. The layout is neat and the use of color restrained, but we simply don't have enough information to know what this viz is meant to show us. Charts usually end up this simple and unclear for one of two reasons: The chart maker was either striving for well-designed simplicity but failed in execution, or was making assumptions about what the audience already knows. Indeed, this chart may make perfect sense to someone who has been analyzing housing data, but that person will end up having to explain it to a confused audience that's not as familiar with the topic.

1. 1. *The values on the y-axis are unclear.* 40 and –40 what? Deviation from historical what? Limiting the words in labels is good—but limiting them so much that we don't know what the values represent is not.

    2. *The bars are different colors, but it's not immediately clear why.* If we study for a moment, we may get it—they represent regions—but it's unclear enough to give us pause.

    3. *The amount of eye travel needed to connect a bar and its label is very high and, given the width of the chart and the orientation of the labels, very difficult without sliding a finger across.* That also makes the job of connecting color to region harder.

    4. *The headline mentions house prices and income but we see neither anywhere on the chart.* Headlines should reflect the idea people will see or the point you want to discuss. They are neutral when they simply describe the structure of the chart. They are downright obfuscating when they mention variables we can't even find on the chart.

2. This challenge would have been impossible if we hadn't given you the context provided. Once you have that extra information, the adjustments can be made without much structural change. Most of my adjustments focused on text; a little more text goes a long way here. First, I've made the y-axis label more explicit—the

bars represent deviations from normal—and it's now clear that the axis refers to percentages. This is quite a long axis label, but I can't think of a way to make it more succinct.

THE HOUSE PRICE–TO-INCOME RATIO IS OUT OF WHACK, AGAIN

This key indicator dipped where the housing crisis hit hardest. In other markets, it shot up, signaling another possible bubble.

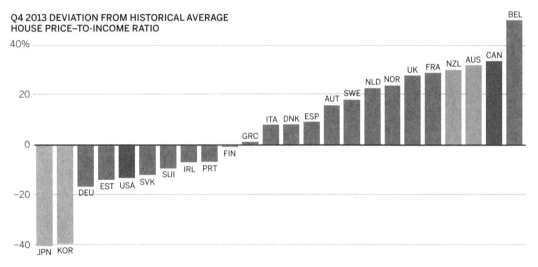

Q4 2013 DEVIATION FROM HISTORICAL AVERAGE
HOUSE PRICE–TO-INCOME RATIO

SOURCE: OECD AND IMF CALCULATIONS

Likewise, I changed the headline to something much more useful. It mentions the key metric—the ratio—and comments on it in a way that confirms what we see in the chart. With so many diving bars and shooting bars, things don't seem in whack. Dynamic change is occurring. I also added a subtitle to give just a little more context that will facilitate discussion. In fact, one good way to create subtitles if you need them is to think of what you'd say about the chart during a presentation. For versions you won't be presenting, that sentence or two will provide valuable context, as it does here: We're not showing this data just because it's interesting; we're showing it because although some countries are still recovering from a housing bubble, others seem headed for another one. That's out of whack!

Normally, I advocate for fewer words on a chart, but in the absence of changing the form, this one was too simple and required more. This version has added words but it doesn't feel more complex. That's in part because of the left alignment of text and because the labels are all horizontal now as well, and snug to the bars. The sideways words and the difficulty in connecting labels to bars were two of the elements that most frustrated me with the original. The connection between value and country is now much clearer—so I decided to keep the color groupings. It's not hard here to pick out the North American countries, the European countries, and so forth. (But I waffled on this; removing those colors wouldn't be a bad choice either.)

Finally, you may not have noticed, but this chart is wider than the original. I did that deliberately to create breathing room. In some ways the tightly packed tall and thin bars are more visually dynamic, but they cause problems with the labels. And when I decided that I needed more words, I thought more horizontal space would keep those words from turning into blocks of text that overwhelmed the visual. It's subtle but clarifying.

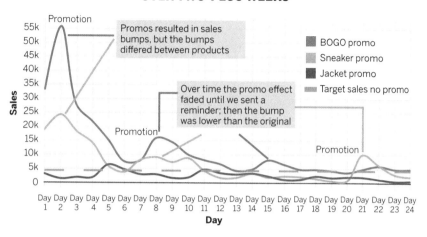

**STORE PROMOTIONS AND SALES
OVER TWO-PLUS WEEKS**

Promotion

Promos resulted in sales bumps, but the bumps differed between products

- BOGO promo
- Sneaker promo
- Jacket promo
- Target sales no promo

Promotion

Over time the promo effect faded until we sent a reminder; then the bump was lower than the original

Promotion

Sales: 55k, 50k, 45k, 40k, 35k, 30k, 25k, 20k, 15k, 10k, 5k, 0

Day 1 Day 2 Day 3 Day 4 Day 5 Day 6 Day 7 Day 8 Day 9 Day 10 Day 11 Day 12 Day 13 Day 14 Day 15 Day 16 Day 17 Day 18 Day 19 Day 20 Day 21 Day 22 Day 23 Day 24

Day

THE OVERDONE LINE CHART

I wish this kind of chart were less common than it is. It seems to pop up especially when the goal is to show viewers not just the data but also an analysis of it. When it comes time to provide the takeaway, the chart maker seems to lose trust in the visual and fill it with words and marks to ensure that the audience knows where to look to see the analysis. Unfortunately, all the words and marks here don't create clarity; they leach it out. We don't know whether we should be looking or reading, and with all those places to focus, it's unclear where to start. Let's work on it.

1. Identify at least two instances of redundancy and say how you'd eliminate them.
2. Identify at least three more elements that make the chart less clear than it could be.
3. Sketch a clearer version that maintains focus on all three variables. Assume that the y-axis refers to dollars. Assume that the promo schedule is as follows:

Day 1: Original promo
Day 5: Follow-up email 1
Day 14: Follow-up email 2
Day 20: Last-chance email

4. Sketch a version of this chart that focuses clearly on a comparison of sneaker and jacket promotions.
5. Sketch a version that shows the "valuable" promotion period versus the "costly" promotion period (assuming that your analysis showed that promotional activities after 12 days were not cost-beneficial).

(sketch space)

DISCUSSION

Too much content and too much redundancy make this chart overdone. Visual elements that aren't part of the actual data visualization, trend lines that fight for attention—it's hard to know where to focus. The redundancy also contributes to a lack of focus. Redundancy isn't a good thing, but it can be instructive. We tend to repeat what we think is important. To make sure the audience gets it, we chart it, label it, point to it, give it color, caption it. If you can identify redundancy, it may mean you've found the ideas you want to highlight and you just need to bring them forward in other ways that don't create clutter and confusion.

1. 1. *The x-axis labels.* Repeating "day" 24 times clutters up the page and makes it hard to see which day connects to which vertical grid line once the numbers are in double digits. Furthermore, the axis itself does the job of telling us what the values 1 through 24 are. You could also consider not putting every day on the x-axis. Ask yourself whether it's important that the audience be able to access every day's value. If it's not—if, say, only the days that email promotions went out are important—you could eliminate most of these labels altogether.

   2. *Promotion "bumps" captions.* The words in the caption boxes describe what we see in the line chart and also point to what they describe, where there are other labels. So we've shown a bump, talked about a bump, pointed to the bump, and labeled the bump. The bump seems important, but so much information around it makes it harder to use. Should I look at the chart? Read the caption? Start with the labels? Which pointers should I start with? There's no clear way through this chart because of the redundancy.

   3. *The headline.* This headline describes the structure of the chart: store promotions (points along the trend line) and sales (y-axis) over two-plus weeks (x-axis). Remember that users usually don't read from the headline down—they start with the visual field and use the headline as a "confirming cue" to check whether what they think they see is in fact what they're being shown. Use your headline to describe the main idea of a chart, not its structure.

2. 1. *The y-axis.* It needs more information. Is this dollars? Units? What?

2. *The grid lines.* Their heaviness and number distract from the trend lines. Grid lines are most valuable when you want the audience to be able to map values anywhere along the x-axis to the y-axis. In other words, if specific points on the trend line are important, grid lines will help. Ask how many x-axis points need to be accessed on the y-axis: One every week? Every day? (If individual points are more important than the general trend, perhaps a trend line isn't the right form. Maybe a dot plot or a table would serve you better.) If the trend line matters most, the grid lines can go, along with the visual noise they create.

3. *Color.* The color scheme of the trend lines is perfectly fine, but the additional colors on the page create confusion. The thick teal of the target-sales line gives it too much prominence, and the dashes make an already busy grid busier. This is secondary information, for reference. A thin gray would work better. The dark-gray caption boxes draw our eyes, so we fight between looking at the chart and reading the captions. They also add to an overall heaviness.

4. *Pointers.* Although they're effective in connecting captions to the bumps described, they create confusion by crossing over lines and using color. The various shapes and angles lessen clarity and create unnecessary eye travel.

5. *Alignment.* There is none. Labels float; captions are offset; the key is on its own plane. So many unique entry points erode clarity.

3. This chart makes an exponential leap in clarity without losing any crucial information. Maybe surprisingly, most of the newfound clarity comes from simply removing some elements and aligning others. I took away all the grid lines except those for the promo days. Yes, this creates a cleaner look—but more important, it helps us see the story. Now the distance between two vertical lines represents the life of a promo email. We instantly see each bump and how it weakens over time until the next promo. Captions have been replaced with a subtitle that provides the same information in just seven words, with no pointers and no dark-gray boxes. And the title and subtitle are confirming cues, reminding viewers what they've just seen in the chart.

Alignment is on two verticals: the y-axis and the key. The target line is quieter—a reference point rather than a primary visual feature.

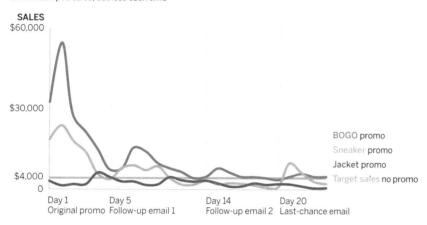

THE LONG-TAIL LIFE OF STORE PROMOTIONS

Emails bumped sales, but less each time

SALES
$60,000

$30,000

BOGO promo
Sneaker promo
Jacket promo
Target sales no promo

$4,000
0

Day 1   Day 5   Day 14   Day 20
Original promo Follow-up email 1 Follow-up email 2 Last-chance email

4. Often, once you heighten a chart's clarity, you can see a number of ways to create variations on the theme. In this case, I used all the same techniques as in the previous challenge, but I also "zoomed in." The y-axis goes only to $30,000. I could have just removed the orange BOGO line from the original, but that would have left half the vertical space empty. Making the y-axis half as high doubled the change between two points in the space, so the curves are more pronounced. For this comparison, that's useful. Look at how flat the blue and pink lines are on the previous chart compared with this one.

A note of caution: Juxtaposing this chart with the previous one would not be a good idea. It would create confusion because the audience would want to compare the charts to each other. The blue line in the second chart looks a lot like the orange one in the first, even though it represents much less change. So give each of these charts its own space. Don't invite comparison on different scales.

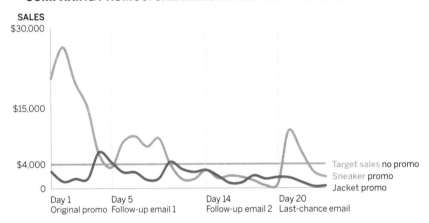

COMPARING PROMOS: SNEAKERS DID BETTER THAN JACKETS

5. Once again, here's a variation on the theme; this one divides the space according to the analysis. Labels make the delineation clear. I removed the labels from the costly-time promos while adding one (Day 12) for the demarcation between the two regions. That wasn't necessary; I just thought it emphasized that anything following the valuable time should be downplayed. I also downplayed low-value time by fading the color—signaling to the audience that this is not where their focus should be. The headline describes the idea authoritatively.

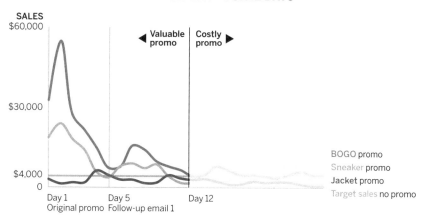

STORE PROMOTIONS ARE WORTH IT—FOR 12 DAYS

THE HOT MESS OF A HEAT MAP

A heat map's strength is also its weakness. It relies on color change—rather than the more typical size or distance—to show difference. That's powerful because it creates regions with similar coloring, forming "hot spots" (or, depending on the variables, "cold spots") that tell us something about regional and clustered relationships in a way that other forms can't. It may be one of the few chart types that stays clear even when you squint. However, color gradations aren't easy to get right. In general, seeing meaningful differences between colors is more difficult than dissecting spatial relationships. And because they often include lots of data, heat maps must be well organized to be clear. When they work, they sing. But executed poorly, they appear random, like this one. The colors are dynamic and eye-catching, but it's hard to discern meaning in this patchwork. Let's work on it.

1. Describe how this visualization's axes are organized and identify at least two alternative ways to organize them.
2. Sketch a new version of it using a different organizing principle.
3. Describe the general color scheme of this heat map.
4. Sketch a new version using a different color scheme to improve clarity.

IN-DEMAND SKILLS IN 15 BUSINESS FUNCTIONS

Some skills matter much more than others based on nearly 25 million job postings collected between September 2014 and August 2015.

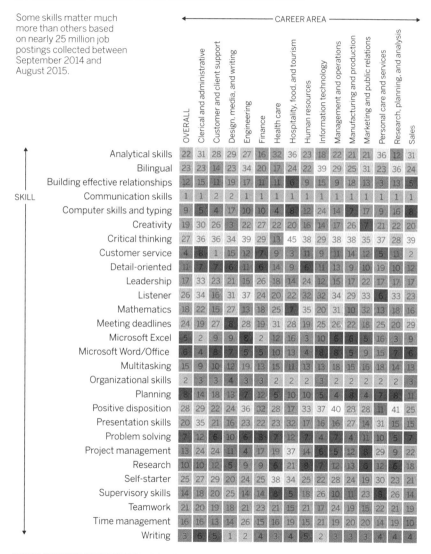

SOURCE: "THE HUMAN FACTOR," BY BURNING GLASS TECHNOLOGIES, NOVEMBER 2015

(sketch space)

DISCUSSION

There's a method to the madness here. The information is organized systematically, and colors are meant to distinguish rankings. Hot spots and cold spots are here, sort of, but finding them takes work. The general sense of randomness results from arbitrary principles used to sort the information. It's organized, but it's still unclear. To increase clarity, you need to understand how it was sorted in the first place and then find a new set of organizing principles.

1. The x-axis is alphabetical by job sector save the first column, which represents overall ranking for each skill—presumably an average of all the others. That makes sense. Putting "Overall" amid the different jobs that make up the overall score would seem strange. We're used to getting the full score first or last.

   X-axis alternative grouping 1: by job type—health care, finance, manufacturing, management, etc. Organizing this way would show whether in-demand (or low-demand) skills cluster within job sectors.

   X-axis alternative grouping 2: by median salary. If we ranked these from highest to lowest median salary, we could see how in-demand (and low-demand) skills cluster around high-paying and low-paying jobs.

   Both are valid groupings, but neither is so compelling that it makes me want to adopt it. The job types are already rather broad; creating even broader groupings seems superfluous and probably wouldn't add to the clarity. Median salaries sound like a good idea, but the salary range within information technology, for example, is enormous. The median salaries may not be that different from one another. After I've thought this through, I may just leave it as is.

   The y-axis is also alphabetical, by skill. This feels arbitrary and problematic. Skills are specific enough that they can be grouped with more purpose than this.

Alternative grouping 1: by skill type. Skills could be clustered in "leadership," "technical," "intellectual," "collaborative," and so forth. If hot spots emerged within some of those clusters, we would immediately see whether certain categories are more highly valued than others.

Alternative grouping 2: by ranking. This seems almost too obvious to overlook. The list of skills can descend from overall ranking 1 to overall ranking 28. That ensures that the hot spots are at the top and the cold spots at the bottom. We then have a map that can be traversed easily from "skills in demand" to "skills less valued."

2. The allure of organizing skills by overall ranking was irresistible, so I used that. It paid immediate dividends. Now we see the hot-to-cold skills and we can pick out some outliers—gray amid the color and color amid the gray. I didn't change the x-axis, because other possible ways of arranging the information didn't feel compelling enough. This looks like an improvement on the original, but color is still an issue.

3. What appeared to be haphazard color in the original was actually carefully planned. When the skills are rank-ordered, we see it: 1–2 yellows; 3–4 oranges; 5–6 reds; 7–8 purples; 9–10 blues. After that the gray gets lighter as the ranking goes down. It's a reasonable attempt at a deliberate color scheme, but it doesn't quite work. For one thing, red is more dominant than orange or yellow—"hotter"—but it represents a lower ranking. And because the blue is significantly separate from the redness of the rest of the palette, it draws the eye even though it represents the lowest of the top 10 rankings.

THE MOST IN-DEMAND SKILLS IN 15 BUSINESS FUNCTIONS

Derived from nearly 25 million job postings collected between September 2014 and August 2015.

CAREER AREA

SKILL BY OVERALL RANK

	OVERALL	Clerical and administrative	Customer and client support	Design, media, and writing	Engineering	Finance	Health care	Hospitality, food, and tourism	Human resources	Information technology	Management and operations	Manufacturing and production	Marketing and public relations	Personal care and services	Research, planning, and analysis	Sales
Communication skills	1	1	2	2	2	1	1	1	1	1	1	1	1	1	1	1
Organizational skills	2	3	3	4	3	3	2	2	2	3	2	2	2	2	3	3
Writing	3	6	5	1	2	4	3	4	5	2	3	3	3	4	4	4
Customer service	4	8	1	15	12	7	9	3	11	9	11	14	12	5	11	2
Microsoft Excel	5	2	9	9	8	2	12	16	3	10	6	6	5	16	3	9
Microsoft Word/Office	6	4	8	7	5	5	10	13	4	8	8	5	9	15	7	6
Problem solving	7	12	6	10	6	8	7	12	7	4	7	4	11	10	5	7
Planning	8	14	18	13	7	12	5	10	10	5	4	8	4	7	8	11
Computer skills and typing	9	5	4	17	10	10	4	8	12	24	14	7	17	9	16	8
Research	10	10	12	5	9	9	6	21	8	7	12	13	6	12	6	18
Detail oriented	11	7	7	6	11	6	14	9	11	13	9	10	19	10	12	
Building effective relationships	12	15	11	19	17	11	11	6	9	15	9	18	13	3	13	5
Project management	13	24	24	11	4	17	19	37	14	6	5	12	8	29	9	22
Supervisory skills	14	18	20	25	14	14	8	5	18	26	10	11	23	8	26	14
Multitasking	15	9	10	12	9	13	15	11	13	13	18	15	16	14	14	13
Time management	16	16	13	14	26	15	9	15	21	19	20	20	14	19	10	
Leadership	17	33	23	21	15	26	14	24	12	15	17	22	17	17	17	
Mathematics	18	22	15	27	13	18	25	7	35	20	31	10	32	13	18	16
Creativity	19	30	26	3	22	27	22	20	16	14	17	26	7	21	22	20
Presentation skills	20	35	21	16	23	22	23	32	17	16	16	27	14	31	15	15
Teamwork	21	20	19	18	21	23	21	15	21	17	24	19	15	22	19	19
Analytical skills	22	31	28	29	27	16	32	36	23	18	22	21	21	36	12	31
Bilingual	23	23	14	23	34	20	17	24	22	39	29	25	31	23	36	24
Meeting deadlines	24	19	27	8	28	19	31	28	19	25	26	22	18	25	20	29
Self-starter	25	27	29	20	24	25	38	34	25	22	28	24	19	30	23	21
Listener	26	34	16	31	37	24	20	22	32	32	34	29	33	6	33	23
Critical thinking	27	36	36	34	39	29	13	45	38	29	38	38	35	37	28	39
Positive disposition	28	29	22	24	36	32	28	17	33	37	40	28	28	11	41	25

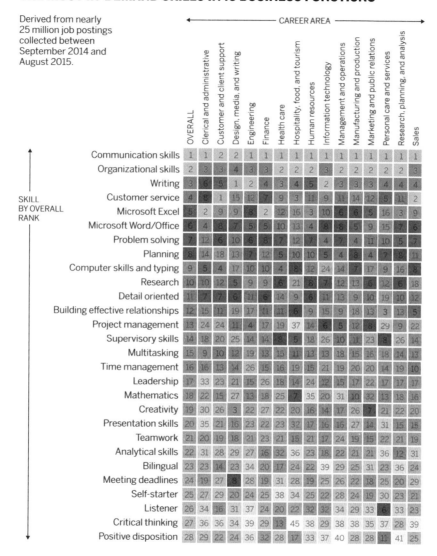

SOURCE: "THE HUMAN FACTOR," BY BURNING GLASS TECHNOLOGIES, NOVEMBER 2015

4. Two key changes bring clarity to this heat map. First, the top 10 skills are all blue, with decreasing saturation as scores decline. Because skill ratings are of a piece, there's no need to use highly contrasting colors for rankings. A score of 9 is not so different from a score of 4 that one needs to be orange and the other blue. By using a single color, I created a single source of "heat": the color blue, with darker blue representing "hotter" spots, or higher rankings. You might argue that blue means "cool" and maybe isn't the best choice for a single color here. Fair critique. In this case the blue isn't in opposition to anything, and rankings aren't particularly associated with a "hot" metaphor (they're more about high and low), so I'm OK with using blue. But I would understand if you chose red or orange.

Second, I flipped gray to move from light to dark rather than dark to light. An interim version of this chart (not pictured here) didn't flip the gray, and it created a contrast between the very light blue of something ranked 10 and the dark gray of something ranked 11. That didn't make as much sense to me as moving from light blue to light gray. Looking down the list of overall rankings in this version, we see a natural gradient effect: dark colors are the extremes, and light colors are the middle.

As a bonus, I made two more small adjustments that didn't appear in the published version to improve the clarity of this heat map. I separated the overall column from the rest, so it now serves as part of the skill label, an inline key. Metaphorically, it makes sense to separate it from the other categories, since it comprises them. I also created space between the top 10 skills and the rest. To consider 28 skills all together is somewhat overwhelming. By dividing them, I effectively created two charts: "The Most Important Skills" and "The Rest." It's subtle, but that little cross-section of white space helps immensely.

TOP SKILLS REQUIRED IN 15 BUSINESS FUNCTIONS

Not surprising: Communication is crucial. Surprising: Teamwork doesn't crack the top 20.

	OVERALL	Clerical and administrative	Customer and client support	Design, media, and writing	Engineering	Finance	Health care	Hospitality, food, and tourism	Human resources	Information technology	Management and operations	Manufacturing and production	Marketing and public relations	Personal care and services	Research, planning, and analysis	Sales
Communication skills	1	1	2	2	1	1	1	1	1	1	1	1	1	1	1	1
Organizational skills	2	3	3	4	3	3	2	2	2	3	2	2	2	2	2	3
Writing	3	6	5	1	2	4	3	4	5	2	3	3	3	4	4	4
Customer service	4	8	1	15	12	7	9	3	11	9	11	14	12	5	11	2
Microsoft Excel	5	2	9	9	8	2	12	16	3	10	6	6	5	16	3	9
Microsoft Word/Office	6	4	8	7	5	5	10	13	4	8	8	5	9	15	7	6
Problem solving	7	12	6	10	6	8	7	12	7	4	7	4	11	10	5	7
Planning	8	14	18	13	7	12	5	10	10	5	4	8	4	7	8	11
Computer skills and typing	9	5	4	17	10	10	4	8	12	24	14	7	17	9	16	8
Research	10	10	12	5	9	9	6	21	8	7	12	13	6	12	6	18
Detail oriented	11	7	7	6	11	6	14	9	6	11	13	9	10	19	10	12
Building effective relationships	12	15	11	19	17	11	11	6	9	15	9	18	13	3	13	5
Project management	13	24	24	11	4	17	19	37	14	6	5	12	8	29	9	22
Supervisory skills	14	18	20	25	14	14	8	5	18	26	10	11	23	8	26	14
Multitasking	15	9	10	12	19	13	15	11	13	13	18	15	16	18	14	13
Time management	16	16	13	14	26	15	16	19	15	21	19	20	20	14	19	10
Leadership	17	33	23	21	15	26	18	14	24	12	15	17	22	17	17	17
Mathematics	18	22	15	27	13	18	25	7	35	20	31	10	32	13	18	16
Creativity	19	30	26	3	22	27	22	20	16	14	17	26	7	21	22	20
Presentation skills	20	35	21	16	23	22	23	32	17	16	16	27	14	31	15	15
Teamwork	21	20	19	18	21	23	21	15	21	17	24	19	15	22	21	19
Analytical skills	22	31	28	29	27	16	32	36	23	18	22	21	21	36	12	31
Bilingual	23	23	14	23	34	20	17	24	22	39	29	25	31	23	36	24
Meeting deadlines	24	19	27	8	29	9	31	28	19	25	26	22	18	25	20	29
Self-starter	25	27	29	20	24	25	38	34	25	22	28	24	19	30	23	21
Listener	26	34	16	31	37	24	20	22	32	32	34	29	33	6	33	23
Critical thinking	27	36	36	34	39	29	13	45	38	29	38	38	35	37	28	39
Positive disposition	28	29	22	24	36	32	28	17	33	37	40	28	28	11	41	25

SOURCE: "THE HUMAN FACTOR," BY BURNING GLASS TECHNOLOGIES, NOVEMBER 2015.
RANKINGS BASED ON 25 MILLION JOB POSTINGS COLLECTED BETWEEN SEPTEMBER 2014 AND AUGUST 2015.

CHAPTER 3

CHOOSING CHART TYPES

"Am I allowed to use pie charts?"   —Anonymous workshop attendee

THE QUOTE ON THE PREVIOUS PAGE IS REAL, and it's disappointing that anyone would feel such trepidation. It demonstrates how fraught choosing a chart type can become. We stress about making the *right* choice because we live in an age when charts draw comment and even derision on the social web. Just as the grammar police like to make fun of poor sentences, visual grammarians are ready to pounce when charts don't meet their rules for proper chart making.

Forget all that. It's destructive, not constructive, criticism. And although there are a few rules you should know and try to follow, most of them are actually just conventions. When it comes to choosing what kind of chart you'll make, the ends ought to justify the means. If it clearly conveys the idea you want your audience to come away with, use it.

Is there a right and a wrong choice between the following charts?

Most likely not. We could create contexts in which one version would be better than the other, but if the idea is to highlight the two large pieces, both are *effective enough*.

Follow these guidelines when considering chart type.

1 **Know the basic categories.** The simplest way to begin is to understand your intent. Are you:

- Making a comparison?
- Showing a distribution?
- Showing proportions?
- Mapping something?
- Showing a nonstatistical concept?

If you know the answer, you've already narrowed down your choices. For example, if you're showing a proportion, you know that a line chart won't work but a stacked area or a stacked bar might. Consult the chart selection tool in appendix B to see which types are most common for each of these tasks. Use that diagram as a *starting point.* You can also try other types that don't appear there. Remember that some chart types can achieve multiple intents. Two stacked bars next to each other, for example, can make a proportional comparison.

2 **Listen to how you describe things.** Find someone to chat with about your data and the idea you want to convey. Listen to your own words and jot some down—you might say something that describes the type of chart best suited to your data. You might hear yourself say, "The individual years don't matter as much as the trend over the years." You've just suggested a line chart that shows a trend instead of a bar chart that plots yearly values. Or you might say, "There was a huge gap between expectations and performance." That could lead you to try a form that can literally show a huge gap, such as a dot plot. You'll be surprised at how often words you use to describe your intent lead you directly to a chart type. To help you, I've included a glossary of types matched to some of the words associated with those approaches. See appendix C.

3 **Rely on your workhorses.** Cleverness is overvalued, in life and in chart making. In an effort to be noticed, we sometimes try unusual chart forms, such as forced-directed networks or alluvials. They have a place in your toolbox, but don't push it. Most dataviz challenges can be handled by three chart types and their variants:

- Line charts (stacked area, slope graph)
- Bar charts (stacked bar, dot plot)
- Scatter plots (bubble chart, histogram)

Make sure you have a good reason to move beyond the basics. Understand that more-specialized and unusual chart types will require more effort on the part of your viewers. It may be helpful to give them an explanation of how it works or a simple prototype.

4 **Don't forget tables.** Sometimes all the individual data points in a set matter more than a trend or what comprises them. In such cases a table may be the best option. Tables may also work for very small sets of data—say, three points in two categories—when visualizing doesn't elucidate any larger point and would take more time than it's worth. Tables are, in a sense, visualizations: They use predictable proportions of horizontal and vertical space to make data more accessible. And they remain a powerful tool.

5 **Bonus pro tip: Use one axis.** One of my favorite chart types is the less common dot plot. It puts marks on a single axis (a variation is the bubble plot, which puts differently sized bubbles on one axis). Often a dot plot can replace a bar chart to great effect. When your main goal in a bar chart is to compare each variable with the others on the y-axis measurement, a dot plot may make that easier. Why? Because we don't have to scan horizontal space to find the vertical difference between two bars. Try to see the difference in value between variables 2 and 7 in the bar chart and the dot plot:

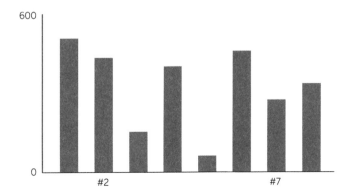 

The dot plot gives a more immediate sense of the difference. You can use one either horizontally or vertically, and it takes up minimal space. Give it a try.

6 **One more note: Good writers are great readers.** Likewise, good chart makers are great chart consumers. Find inspiration in others' visualizations. Any number of sources will provide endless examples. Subscribe to #dataviz on Twitter or r/dataisbeautiful on Reddit. Bookmark sites such as the Upshot from the *New York Times* and the *Economist*'s Graphic Detail blog. Subscribe to newsletters such as *Best in Visual Storytelling*. Mine them for what you like—and for what you don't. Hold a constructive crit session on some of the charts you come across. (I outline a method for doing this in *Good Charts*.) Sketch alternative versions of others' visualizations. The material is out there. Go get it.

Choosing the right chart type is easier than you may think. Focus on bringing your idea forward, whatever type you choose. If it's not working, try a different one. Stress less.

The following challenges are designed to develop skills in picking chart types. Focus mostly on ways to remove confusion and clutter, using the prompts with each chart. For these challenges, think about color, labels, standard conventions, and other considerations only as they relate to choosing chart types.

CHOOSING CHART TYPES WARM-UP

1. Match each chart intent to visual forms that are likely to represent it. (For help, consult the glossary of chart types in appendix A.)

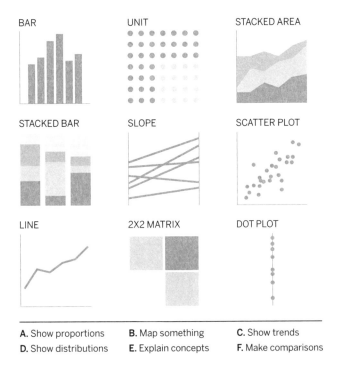

BAR

UNIT

STACKED AREA

STACKED BAR

SLOPE

SCATTER PLOT

LINE

2X2 MATRIX

DOT PLOT

A. Show proportions   **B.** Map something   **C.** Show trends
D. Show distributions   **E.** Explain concepts   **F.** Make comparisons

2. Talking with a colleague about how you might visualize some data, you say, "It's interesting to see how the components make up the total at any given point, but then also how those totals change over time. The shifting proportions say a lot about what's happened."

Highlight key words in this description and choose two chart types that might show what you described.

3. You have five minutes to present to the board. To show how the business has shifted from one revenue mix to another, you could use two stacked bars. But you're thinking of using an alluvial diagram because it's visually arresting and you want to impress the directors. Should you? Why or why not?

4. A slope graph connects two points to form a linear trend line, removing all data from between those two points. Which of these line graphs would be less appropriate to turn into a slope graph? Why?

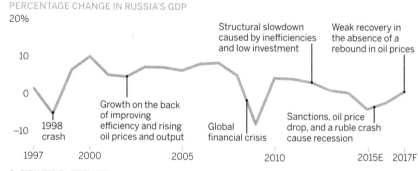

A RUSSIA'S ECONOMIC PERFORMANCE LINKED TO OIL PRICES

Ups and downs follow a predictable pattern.

PERCENTAGE CHANGE IN RUSSIA'S GDP

E = ESTIMATED F = FORECASTED
SOURCE: FRONTIER STRATEGY GROUP

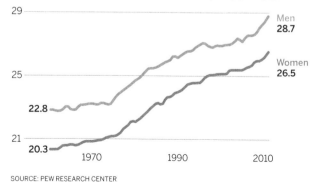

B MEDIAN AGE AT FIRST MARRIAGE, 1960–2011

SOURCE: PEW RESEARCH CENTER

5. A friend wants your help visualizing data. She says, "We're trying to see if there's some correlation between how much money people make and how much they donate. Just glancing at the data, I see a few who seem to give a higher proportion of their income to charity, but I don't know if they're outliers or there's a cluster of them."

   Highlight the visual-related words you heard and say what type of chart you might steer her to.

6. Each of hundreds of entries in a data set includes the following information:

   - Name
   - Department
   - Location
   - Manager name
   - Direct reports' names
   - Direct reports' locations
   - Indirect reports' names
   - Indirect reports' locations
   - Indirect reports' managers
   - Indirect reports' departments

   From this you want to create a visual of managerial structure. What chart type might work for you?

7. In a pitch to VCs, you want to show what you call "a huge chasm" in the market between products and customers' access to them. Your solution, you say, is "the bridge" connecting customers to the products. Which of the following sketches might be a good start for visualizing your value proposition?

A

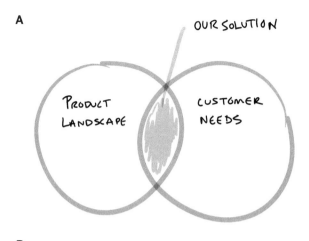

B

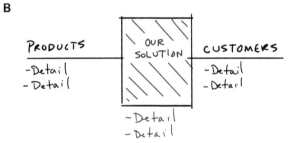

C

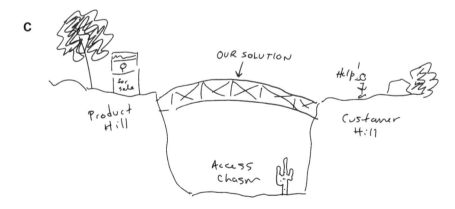

8. A simple data set shows the average number of hours spent in meetings per employee last year and this year at headquarters and in two satellite offices. How might you display this?

9. You want to categorize football players on two dimensions: speed and strength. Each player gets a score for each dimension. What would be a good chart type to map how the players compare with one another?

10. You want to convey how rare on-the-job accidents are in your factories—only 4 employees out of 1,000 have been injured in the past year. What type of visualization might powerfully convey this?

DISCUSSION

1. Answers are shown below each chart. Consult the glossary in appendix A for more on each chart type shown here and for other types.

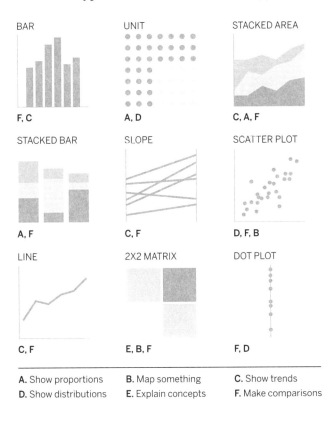

BAR

F, C

UNIT

A, D

STACKED AREA

C, A, F

STACKED BAR

A, F

SLOPE

C, F

SCATTER PLOT

D, F, B

LINE

C, F

2X2 MATRIX

E, B, F

DOT PLOT

F, D

A. Show proportions   **B.** Map something   **C.** Show trends
D. Show distributions   **E.** Explain concepts   **F.** Make comparisons

2. "It's interesting to see how the components make up the total at any given point, but then also how those totals change over time. The shifting proportions say a lot about what's happened."

Chart type 1: Stacked area. It combines proportions to show both how components make up the total and the change over time of a line chart.

Chart type 2: Stacked bar series. If only certain points in time matter, you can place a series of stacked bars side by side as snapshots rather than using the continuous timeline of a stacked area chart.

3. The best answer is "It depends." If the directors have seen alluvial diagrams before and know what to expect, that could be a captivating choice. But if they haven't, it may cause more confusion than it's worth. You'll end up wasting precious time (you only have five minutes!) explaining how it works when you could be talking about ideas in stacked bars—a form they're certain to be familiar with. Also, as with pie charts, the more variables you have, the more complex and less accessible alluvials become as section flows twist over one another. So proceed cautiously.

4. Answer: A. Slope graphs are beautifully simple, but they run the risk of hiding important variation and detail. In B, the marriage chart, the data is nearly linear. Simplifying it

wouldn't violate the spirit of the change. With A, however, a slope chart would obfuscate the most important change. Here is the oil chart as a slope chart, making the failed use case immediately clear.

A RUSSIA'S ECONOMY LINKED TO OIL PRICES

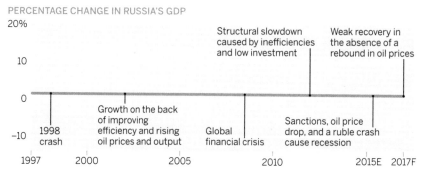

Ups and downs follow a predictable pattern.

PERCENTAGE CHANGE IN RUSSIA'S GDP

E = ESTIMATED F = FORECASTED
SOURCE: FRONTIER STRATEGY GROUP

B MEDIAN AGE AT FIRST MARRIAGE, 1960–2011

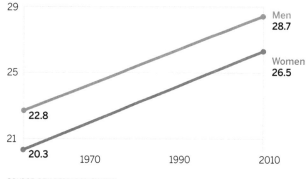

SOURCE: PEW RESEARCH CENTER

5. "We're trying to see if there's some correlation between how much money people make and how much they donate. Just glancing at the data, I see a few who seem to give a higher proportion of their income to charity, but I don't know if they're outliers or there's a cluster of them."

You probably want to try a scatter plot here. Your friend suggested the axes: income and donation. By putting down many dots, you'd create clusters and outliers, and a correlation would be revealed if the scatter moved generally up and to the right—higher income equaling higher donations.

An alternative is a dot plot in which the axis is the ratio between giving and income: A person who gives $1,000 and makes $100,000 would be at 1% on the axis. One who gives $12,000 and makes $100,000 would be at 12% on the axis. And so forth. You would still see clusters and outliers—but if there were too many points to plot, it would be hard to sort out where the clusters were.

6. A network diagram might work well here. Network diagrams usually require special software and some extra configuration and design, lest they become rats' nests of nodes and links. But when done well they can help in sorting complex networks, seeing clusters, and understanding intricacies. In this case using color on the nodes to represent departments and separating departments with space would help highlight which ones are highly interconnected and which are more isolated. It could expose silos in the organization.

7. Answer: B. Conceptual diagrams present their own challenges and pitfalls. Without data controlling the boundaries of a visual, we tend to get creative—often too creative—with metaphors to convey ideas. That's the case here with C, an overdesigned approach that uses metaphors too literally. The idea we want to convey will be subsumed by the metaphor and the detailed decoration. This may look silly, but it's incredibly common. A comes up short because it mixes metaphors. We want to convey the idea of a bridge or a connector, whereas a Venn diagram conveys overlap or commonality—hardly the same thing. B is clearly the most promising start: it shows a connector between two domains.

8. Try a table. With just six data points and no real need to focus on or compare any particular aspects of the data set, it's the quickest and clearest approach. It might look something like this:

	LAST YEAR	THIS YEAR
HQ	510	570
Satellite Office A	325	295
Satellite Office B	300	210

9. Here's a great opportunity to use a two-by-two. The crucial thing is the desire to categorize and map the players. A two-by-two, which crosses the two axes to create regions, is designed to categorize. The dots then map onto the categories. It might look something like this before the players are plotted:

FOOTBALL PLAYERS

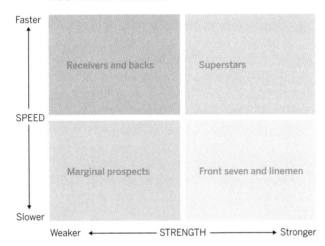

10. A good choice here might be a unit chart. Unit charts use marks, usually dots, to represent some number of actual units. For example, one dot might equal $1,000, or one million widgets, or one death. The advantage of this is that it helps an audience make a stronger connection to a physical entity. Rather than representing a statistic, the unit represents the thing itself. A unit chart is also useful when statistics wouldn't convey an idea well. For example, in this case 4 injuries out of 1,000 is 0.1%. That's a hard value to represent visually other than with a unit chart. Now we not only get a sense of what 0.1% looks like but we see the injuries— and, more important, just how many employees weren't injured:

OUR EXCEPTIONAL SAFETY RECORD

ACCIDENTS PER 1,000
EMPLOYEES THIS YEAR

HOW STUDENTS CONTACT THE REGISTRAR'S OFFICE

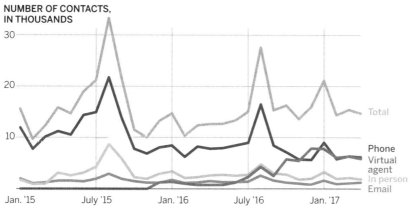

NUMBER OF CONTACTS,
IN THOUSANDS

30

20

10

Total

Phone
Virtual
agent
In person
Email

Jan. '15   July '15   Jan. '16   July '16   Jan. '17

SOURCE: MARK MCCONAHAY

THE SURPRISINGLY ADAPTABLE LINE CHART

A chart type that works well in one context may not work as well in another. This dataviz is serviceable for showing how students contacted the central office at a university overall. But maybe we want to focus on something other than each trend line. Sometimes the best way to make your idea come forward isn't to adjust the chart you have but to try a different chart altogether. Even for a simple data set like this, any number of types and variations on them can be deployed, depending on context. Each challenge here is to sketch an alternative chart type to the line chart above, based on the conversation snippet provided. It may be helpful to highlight visual words and clues in the conversations and to consult the appendixes, where you can find multiple chart types and a matrix that matches visual words to chart types. Let's work on it.

1. "The total number of contacts is important, but it's more important to me that they see how much of that total each category makes up. They'll be able to see shares that make up the whole growing and shrinking over time."

2. "Basically what matters to me is to show how much of the total activity is digital over time. Comparing how those two categories are growing against phone and in-person contacts will tell us where we're going and where we should invest."

3. "I'm worried they'll get lost in all that trend data. Really we just want them to see snapshots of how the mix is changing. Where were we two years ago? Last year? And this year? If they can see those moments, they'll get the idea of how the proportions are changing."

4. "I think if we just give them a snapshot view of digital versus nondigital contacts, year over year, that's enough to get the point across that digital is growing as a total share, and fast."

5. "I want to see the trend line, but it's really busy with all the seasonal spikes. I'd like a simpler view into the trend—is it flat or going up or going down?"

6. "When I analyze the data, I see a different trend than digital versus nondigital. I see that email and in-person contacts are flat, and it's really about the rise of the virtual agent against phone contacts. To just juxtapose those two would really get people to see that new form of contact—virtual agents—shooting up."

(sketch space)

DISCUSSION

The tools we use to make visualizations dissuade us from thinking about what chart type to use. They encourage the "click-and-viz" approach—try one or two until you find one you think works well enough. For example, the original chart looks like standard output from a spreadsheet or a data program. You may think there are no other ways to show this data that will improve on it. Following are six alternatives.

Your charts will improve immeasurably if you get past the click-and-viz impulse and mine your conversations for clues about great ways to make and refine them.

1. "The total number of contacts is important, but it's more important to me that they see how much of that total each category makes up. They'll be able to see shares that make up the whole growing and shrinking over time."

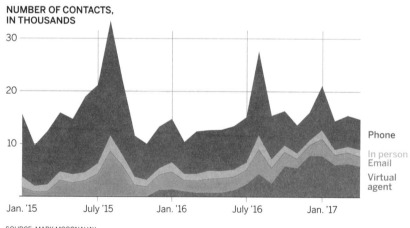

HOW STUDENTS CONTACT THE REGISTRAR'S OFFICE

NUMBER OF CONTACTS,
IN THOUSANDS

SOURCE: MARK MCCONAHAY

This conversation was packed with clues. The talk of parts making up the whole points toward proportional charts, and I considered pies and stacked bars. But neither of those would capture the "over time" as well as a stacked area chart could. This version has an advantage over the basic line chart: instead of plotting each value *against* the others in a way that clusters and tangles lines, we can plot it *with* the others so that they're all discrete and don't fight over space.

2. "Basically what matters to me is to show how much of the total activity is digital over time. Comparing how those two categories are growing against phone and in-person contacts will tell us where we're going and where we should invest."

STUDENTS MOVE TO EMAIL AND VIRTUAL AGENTS

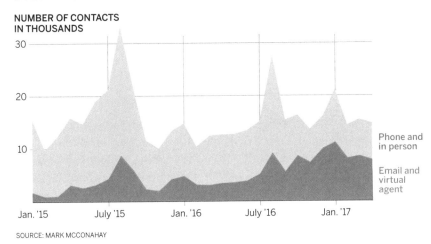

NUMBER OF CONTACTS
IN THOUSANDS

SOURCE: MARK MCCONAHAY

How much . . . over time led me right to the stacked area chart again, because I knew we wanted to see a *total*. The decision to group the categories was dictated by the conversation in which *digital* mattered as a category that didn't exist in the original data set. The focus seemed to be on highlighting digital, so I made its counterpart secondary gray. A line chart may also have worked here.

3. "I'm worried they'll get lost in all that trend data. Really we just want them to see snapshots of how the mix is changing. Where were we two years ago? Last year? And this year? If they can see those moments, they'll get the idea of how the proportions are changing."

HOW STUDENTS CONTACT THE REGISTRAR'S OFFICE

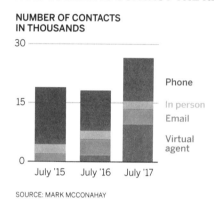

NUMBER OF CONTACTS
IN THOUSANDS

SOURCE: MARK MCCONAHAY

The speaker laid out her chart in the conversation. The words *snapshots* and *moments* led me away from trend lines. But what does she want snapshots of? She said it! Two years ago, last year, and this year. I heard *proportions* again, so I focused on pies or stacked bars. When left with that choice, I usually go with bars, especially if there are more than three variables contained within a proportion and more than one visual to display. Pies are harder to use than bars for making comparisons.

4. "I think if we just give them a snapshot view of digital versus non-digital contacts, year over year, that's enough to get the point across that digital is growing as a total share, and fast."

STUDENTS MOVE TO
EMAIL AND VIRTUAL AGENTS

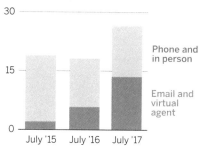

**NUMBER OF CONTACTS
IN THOUSANDS**

Phone and
in person

Email and
virtual
agent

SOURCE: MARK MCCONAHAY

Once again, I heard *snapshots,* and that kept me away from trend lines. *Total share* leads to proportion forms. This version can easily be envisioned as a series of three very simple pies. Evaluating the differences among these variables wouldn't be hampered by a circular form.

5. "I want to see the trend line, but it's really busy with all the seasonal spikes. I'd like a simpler view into the trend—is it flat or going up or going down?"

HOW STUDENTS CONTACT THE REGISTRAR'S OFFICE

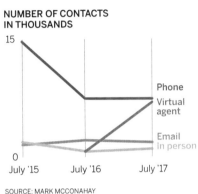

NUMBER OF CONTACTS
IN THOUSANDS

SOURCE: MARK MCCONAHAY

Any time I hear *simple* and *trend* near each other, I think about slope charts. They've gained in popularity recently. They're compact and elegant. They give a greater sense of change over time than bars do, without the noise of all the minor changes in short time spans in a more traditional line chart. But they conceal most of the data. I'm just linking points here. So you should be careful. If those seasonal spikes and many smaller dips and rises are important, a slope chart is a poor choice. Here the slope chart is the first version of this data in which the upward trajectory of virtual agents really stands out. It's a powerfully direct message.

6. "When I analyze the data, I see a different trend than digital versus nondigital. I see email and in-person contacts are flat, and it's really about the rise of the virtual agent against phone contacts. To just juxtapose those two would really get people to see that new form of contact—virtual agents—shooting up."

STUDENTS MOVE TO VIRTUAL AGENTS

NUMBER OF CONTACTS
IN THOUSANDS

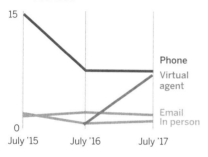

SOURCE: MARK MCCONAHAY

In this case all the language points to a comparison different from what you might have assumed until now was the valuable one. One small change to the previous version—using gray for the flat lines so that they recede—makes it impossible to miss this chart's intent. You can even see that term *shooting up* reflected in the form I chose.

THE CONVOLUTED, TOO CLEVER BY HALF CHART

What do you see? I've heard everything from "padlocks" to "a map of a sewer system" to describe this chart (which is based on a real, published chart, in case you thought I was rigging the challenge with something absurd). Creativity with chart types can be a good thing, and it leads to incredible breakthroughs in understanding if we get it right. But creativity unchecked leads to forms utterly bereft of clarity, and while they may be eye-catching, they're very hard to use. Form is leading function here. It's clear that this chart maker had a plan, but it went awry in a tangle of arrows and labels. Let's work on it.

1. Critique this chart. Understanding that it shows the proportion of people using each platform and the proportion of those who switched from one to the other, explain why you think it's not as effective as it could be. Provide at least three examples.
2. Sketch at least three alternative approaches to charting this data. Choose whatever context you want to highlight.

ANALYTICS, DATA SCIENCE, AND MACHINE LEARNING PLATFORMS

Change from 2016 to 2017

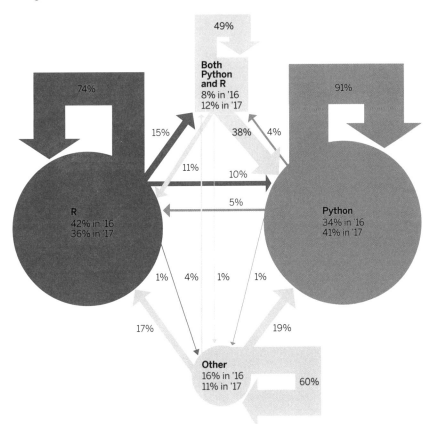

SOURCE: DATA FROM KDNUGGETS.COM

(sketch space)

DISCUSSION

This chart maker was probably thinking about Sankey diagrams (see appendix A). Frustratingly, the visual obscures what is actually straightforward data. We have a year-over-year change of share for four variables and percentage transfers between them. That's it. Why go to such knotty extremes to express it in this more complex way? Usually, to get attention. Initially drawing in an audience is not a trivial concern, and nothing does it faster than a dynamic, colorful data visualization that is unusual in appearance or form. But if it's just eye candy—if it lacks the nutrition of a clear idea—it will leave us with a headache. A common chart type well designed will probably serve us better.

1. *Critique 1: Unclear proportions.* The two circles look proportional, but on the basis of which data—2016 or 2017? The arrows, too, are proportional, it turns out. The width of all the arrows of one color combined would create a 100% stacked bar chart. But those proportions aren't proportional to the circles they shoot out from. And why is the "both" category square while the others are circles—because it comprises two other categories, so it's dissimilar? We don't know.

   Critique 2: Vague labeling. I love minimal labeling, but this is too minimal. For example, what does 91% on the Python arrow represent? It doesn't look like 91% of that circle. Connecting the labels to the arrows helps me understand that it's a percentage transfer—but in fact that transfer is from 2016 values, which aren't shown here! In other words, 91% of 2016 Python users used Python in 2017, but the arrow points back into the 2017 value represented by the circle. Confused? Can't blame you.

   Critique 3: A quiver of arrows. Once this form was chosen, crisscrossing arrows was an inevitable result. To follow one path requires concentration. The effort to keep most of the labels aligned here is actually impressive, but there's no avoiding the complexity inherent in the form. It's hard to see how transfers from one platform to others generally went.

2. I tried six forms and seven charts for this data. Each has its merits and its downsides. I'll discuss them here, working forward from what I think are the least effective.

Pie charts: This challenge effectively shows the limits of pie charts. A sameness to these two sets of proportions makes it hard to see change immediately, and change is all we care about in this context. If I didn't put the percentage values in the pieces, it would be hard to even guesstimate just how much change is represented. What's more, the headline suggests that the change within each platform is probably more important than the overall change between platforms. That is, Python's gains are the cause, and a new set of proportions is the effect. You can probably do better than this.

PYTHON GAINS, R WANES

Data scientists are flocking to Python

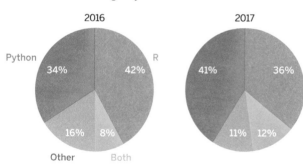

SOURCE: DATA FROM KDNUGGETS.COM

Stacked bars: Stacked bars are somewhat more effective than pie charts in making a middling change accessible. But when they're used for comparison, as here, that change is easiest to spot in the top and bottom pieces, where starting points are shared. The middle pieces float on different starting points, making it somewhat harder to see the change. And, of course, this form still focuses first on the entire composition of platforms, not the change within each. I included two versions to show how one subtle change can improve the effect of the stacked bar. The second version groups the growing pieces together and the shrinking pieces together, giving a more immediate sense that Python and Both are encroaching on R and Other. However, it removes the easy comparison between Python and R, because they're no longer adjacent. Which works best depends on the context. But if comparing Python with R is the context, I would argue that other forms work better than a stacked bar. If we want to see "growing versus shrinking platforms," I like the second stacked bar here.

PYTHON GAINS, R WANES

Data scientists are flocking to Python

USAGE SHARE

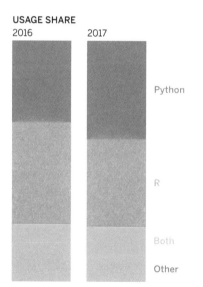

PYTHON GAINS, R WANES

Data scientists are flocking to Python

USAGE SHARE

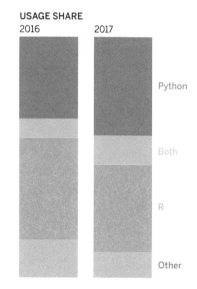

SOURCE: DATA FROM KDNUGGETS.COM

Bar chart: Where pies make it hard to compare one platform year to year, bars make it easy—at the expense of seeing the overall proportion of platforms being used. That might be OK. This is beautifully straightforward. I see that Python is higher than it was, and R is lower, and if that's my context, as the headline suggests, I've hit on a good chart. The organization of the bars also has the neat effect of offsetting the two major groups from the two minor groups.

PYTHON GAINS, R WANES

Data scientists are flocking to Python

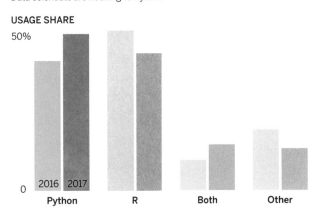

SOURCE: DATA FROM KDNUGGETS.COM

Slope chart: Although I'm plotting the exact same information I did in the bar chart, the lines communicate something different. The bars communicate a binary comparison of two points in time; the slopes suggest a directional trend over time. In the bars, R's share *dropped*. Here, it's *going down*. Notice the difference in those verb tenses: one is complete, and the other is ongoing. You can almost imagine the lines continuing on into the future. And the slopes show Python *crossing over* or *passing* R. In most other ways, this communicates the same idea the bar chart does, and it makes the "major players" and "minor players" distinction as well. If that's our context, it would work well.

PYTHON GAINS, R WANES

Data scientists are flocking to Python

USAGE SHARE

SOURCE: DATA FROM KDNUGGETS.COM

Table: None of the forms so far have shown how this reshaping of the proportions is happening—something the original chart attempted to show. In many contexts that would be the most crucial data—not that a change occurred, but who's moving where. In trying to envision alternative forms for the original chart, I first deconstructed it into a data spreadsheet. I stared at it, thinking, *This works*. Why a table and not a visualization? First, there's not that much data—20 points total in two clusters: shares and transfers. Second, it's clear and comprehensive. If my audience has even a few minutes to spend with the data, I can give them all of it. If I were presenting in front of a room, I probably wouldn't use this, because it would set the group off reading instead of listening to me. I could, however, present it and then use some kind of highlight to draw attention to one or two crucial points of focus.

THE CHANGING LANDSCAPE OF ANALYTICS PLATFORMS
Data scientists are flocking to Python

% SHARE

	2016	2017
Python	34	41
R	42	36
Both	8	12
Other	16	11

% TRANSFER OF SHARE

	From Python	From R	From Both	From Other
To Python		10	38	19
To R	5		11	17
To Both	4	15		4
To Other	1	1	1	

SOURCE: DATA FROM KDNUGGETS.COM

Alluvial diagram: The following is my favorite expression of this data. I find this alluvial to be the best combination of comparing simple proportions (with the bars on each side) and effectively communicating transfers of value from one group to another (through the curves). The transfers are proportional to the total. The "arrows" (in this case, flows) do real work, giving a good sense of just how many people are leaving R for Python, or adding Python to R, and so forth. Also, although the curves crisscross, they have an orderliness that makes them easy to follow.

PYTHON GAINS, R WANES

Data scientists are flocking to Python

USAGE SHARE

2016   2017

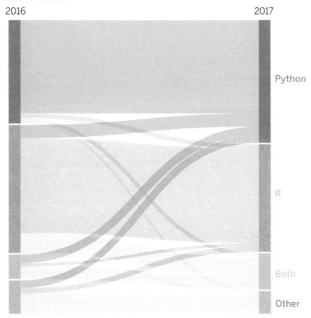

Python

R

Both

Other

SOURCE: DATA FROM KDNUGGETS.COM

This is not a typical form. I arrived at it because of the sense of *transfer* in the original. If you hear words like *flows* and *from here to there* and *flocking from . . . to,* you might want to sketch an alluvial to see whether it will work. The tool used to create this is a simple one called Raw (rawgraphs.io), but other tools, including Plot.ly and Tableau, and programming libraries such as R and D3, can make alluvials as well. They are cousins of Sankey diagrams. Alluvials tend to have all flows connect through all steps, whereas Sankeys tend to show more-complex network flows with multiple termini.

THE GREAT WHISKY CHALLENGE

Sometimes we don't start with a visual; we just have some data. These tables list whiskys and some of their key attributes. Now we need to turn the data into a visualization. That's it. Let's work on it.

Think about how the data is naturally organized and ways you might manipulate that organizing principle: Does the data lend itself to any particular form? A timeline? A map? A scatter plot? Then put the data aside and try to describe it to someone. Tell him or her what you'd like to show with it. Encourage questions. Listen for those keywords that may spark a visual approach. Then sketch what you come up with until you like the way you're approaching the challenge. When you think you've got it, make a neat paper prototype that suggests what the final chart will look like, approximating real values, colors, and labels.

Next try the following challenges based on other people's conversations. Read the conversations, highlight the key words and phrases, and sketch possible approaches according to what was said.

1. "The range of flavors for me was really interesting."

    "How so?"
    "These descriptions like citrusy, peppery, biscuity, even medicinal—the range of flavors and how they interact is interesting."

    "But how do they interact?"
    "That's the thing. Everything is basically some cross between whether the whisky is light or rich and whether it's delicate or smoky. If you know how those two things are interacting, you get all these regions of different flavor combinations."

    "So you can show which flavor profile a whisky has by knowing that?"
    "Yeah, they have a score on each spectrum. But I think showing how the flavors interact, those descriptions, are most interesting. I mean, plotting them in the background might be

	AGE (YEARS)	COST (£/LITRE)	DELICATE TO SMOKY / LIGHT TO RICH (0 TO 10)
ISLAY			
Ardberg	10	60	9.8 / 1.2
Bowmore	12	51	7.6 / 6.3
Bruichladdich	15	171	5.4 / 6.2
Bunnahabhain	12	63	2.8 / 6.6
Caol Ila	12	63	8.8 / 4.1
Lagavulin	16	79	9.2 / 7.7
Lagavulin Distillers	0	570	8.8 / 9.4
Laphroaig	10	58	9.2 / 2.3
HIGHLAND			
anCnoc	12	44	4.2 / 3.4
Arran	10	50	3.8 / 3.9
Arran	14	63	4.2 / 4.8
Dalwhinnie	15	56	4.9 / 3.4
Glenmorangie Original	0	49	3.4 / 4.9
Glen Ord	12	160	6.9 / 4.2
Highland Park	12	46	7.2 / 6.6
Jura Origin	0	49	3.2 / 3.0
Oban	14	71	5.8 / 4.9
Old Pulteney	12	48	6.2 / 6.2
Royal Lochnagar	12	53	4.0 / 4.0
Talisker	10	55	8.2 / 4.3
Talisker	18	106	7.6 / 7.3

	AGE (YEARS)	COST (£/LITRE)	DELICATE TO SMOKY / LIGHT TO RICH (0 TO 10)
SPEYSIDE			
Balvenie DoubleWood	12	55	3.8 / 7.5
BenRiach	16	93	7.1 / 5.1
Cardhu	12	54	4.6 / 3.8
Cragganmore	12	51	6.0 / 6.4
Cragganmore Distillery	0	83	6.0 / 8.5
Dailuaine	16	79	4.9 / 9.1
Glenfiddich	12	46	2.8 / 8.3
Glenfiddich	15	59	3.4 / 8.8
Glenfiddich	18	99	3.6 / 7.3
Glenfiddich	21	164	3.6 / 9.0
Glenfiddich	30	714	3.9 / 9.3
The Glenlivet	12	65	3.4 / 4.0
The Glenlivet	15	59	2.0 / 7.3
The Glenlivet	18	129	2.6 / 8.9
The Glenlivet	21	269	2.8 / 9.0
The Glenlivet	25	500	3.4 / 9.2
Linkwood	12	67	4.2 / 2.6
Macallan	10	108	4.6 / 9.3
Singleton of Dufftown	12	52	4.9 / 7.3
LOWLAND & CAMPBELTOWN			
Glenkinchie (Lowland)	12	55	3.6 / 2.8
Springbank (Campbeltown)	10	61	7.0 / 2.7

CHARACTER	FLAVOR DESCRIPTION
Rich plus...	
...smoky	Pungent, smoky, peaty richness
...a little smoky	Dried fruit, sherry, richness
...a little delicate	Spiced, woody complexity
...delicate	Nutty, barley, biscuity subtleness

CHARACTER	FLAVOR DESCRIPTION
Light plus...	
...delicate	Floral, herby, grassy freshness
...a little delicate	Fresh fruit, citrus, crispness
...a little smoky	Spiced, stewed fruit, ripeness
...smoky	Medicinal, dry smoke, pepperiness

nice, but I bet a lot of people don't know how the flavor of whisky works. Just seeing those profiles mapped would be nice."

2. "I'm fascinated by how regional whisky is."

"How so?"
"Well, there are five pretty distinct regions, and I have no idea whether any one region is known for any particular flavor profile of whisky."

"How would you figure that out?
"You could just plot them on one axis that shows the smoky-delicate score and one that shows the light-to-rich score and see where they fall."

"So you'd see clusters if one region had one profile?"
"Exactly. Only problem is, there are a lot to plot."

"So?"
"I think it might get busy. It might be easier to read if I did just one at a time."

3. "Wow, the price range of whisky is all over the place. I wonder if the expensive ones have any particular flavor profile."

"What's expensive?"
"Some cost hundreds of pounds per liter. Most are clustered in the 50-to-100-pound price range, but a few are way more than that on the list I have."

"Why would some cost so much more?"
"I think it's to do with age, and probably reputation. I don't know."

"Could you add age to the mix? See whether older ones cost more?"
"I like that. Age versus price."

"Or age versus flavor profile? Do older whiskys tend to settle into a certain type of flavor?"

"Maybe I could do all three? Age, price, and flavor?"

4. "There are a lot of interesting variables here, but I want to focus on simple comparisons."

    "Why?"

    "I think in this case, for this audience, making one comparison at a time will work better. I don't want them sitting there trying to figure out three or four variables at a time during the presentation. I just want to be able to show 'this versus that' and 'that versus this' over and over."

    "So, like, price versus age. Smokiness versus region. So on."

    "Exactly. Nice and simple. One at a time."

(sketch space)

DISCUSSION

I hope this was as much fun for you as it was for me. I tended to focus on one particular form for most of it—a 2x2 scatter plot—but I hope and expect that many of you found other ways into this visual challenge. For me, it was hard not to focus on the two "axes" of flavor in whisky as my core structure—though you'll see that in at least one challenge, I got away from that. I tried to escape the 2x2s, but that kept making things complicated, because I knew I'd then have to express the scores for each taste dimension separately. For example, if I chose a bar chart, each whisky would need a bar for the smoky scale and one for the rich scale.

1. "The range of flavors for me was really interesting."

   "How so?"
   "These descriptions like citrusy, peppery, biscuity, even medicinal—the range of flavors and how they interact is interesting."

   "But how do they interact?"
   "That's the thing. Everything is basically some cross between whether the whisky is light or rich and whether it's delicate or smoky. If you know how those two things are interacting, you get all these regions of different flavor combinations."

   "So you can show which flavor profile a whisky has by knowing that?"
   "Yeah, they have a score on each spectrum. But I think just showing how the flavors interact, those descriptions are most interesting. I mean, plotting them in the background might be nice, but I bet a lot of people don't know how the flavor of whisky works. Just seeing those profiles mapped would be nice."

Not all data visualizations focus on the data points. Here the conversation kept revolving around how these two scales interact, and the chart maker was focused on flavor descriptions. The two big clues here were *cross between* and *regions*. Once I decided not to plot specific whisky scores, I focused on a more general approach to mapping the flavors in sectors. Often with 2x2s, creating definitions for the quadrants helps set up a visual space before you plot data on it. In presentations especially, it can be useful to show the blank canvas before filling it. Here, as a visual flourish, I plotted the data lightly in the background. It could be viewed as merely decoration, but it also suggests that whiskys will be found all over this map.

THE WHISKY MAP

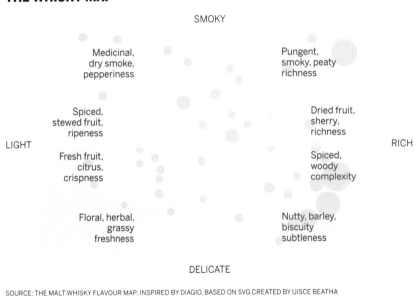

SMOKY

Medicinal, dry smoke, pepperiness

Pungent, smoky, peaty richness

Spiced, stewed fruit, ripeness

Dried fruit, sherry, richness

LIGHT

RICH

Fresh fruit, citrus, crispness

Spiced, woody complexity

Floral, herbal, grassy freshness

Nutty, barley, biscuity subtleness

DELICATE

SOURCE: THE MALT WHISKY FLAVOUR MAP: INSPIRED BY DIAGIO, BASED ON SVG CREATED BY UISCE BEATHA

2. "I'm fascinated by how regional whisky is."

"How so?"

"Well there are five pretty distinct regions and I have no idea whether any one region is known for any particular flavor profile of whisky."

"How would you figure that out?

"You could just plot them on one axis that shows the smoky-delicate score and one that shows the light-to-rich score and see where they fall."

"So you'd see clusters if one region had one profile?"

"Exactly. Only problem is, there are a lot to plot."

"So?"

"I think it might get busy. It might be easier to read if I did just one at a time."

Sketching this confirmed the busyness of plotting everything together, but using colors to code regions felt like a good approach, because there are only five, and only three have more than one data point. The map as a key adds a layer of geographical information that's nice, but a simpler dot key would have been fine too.

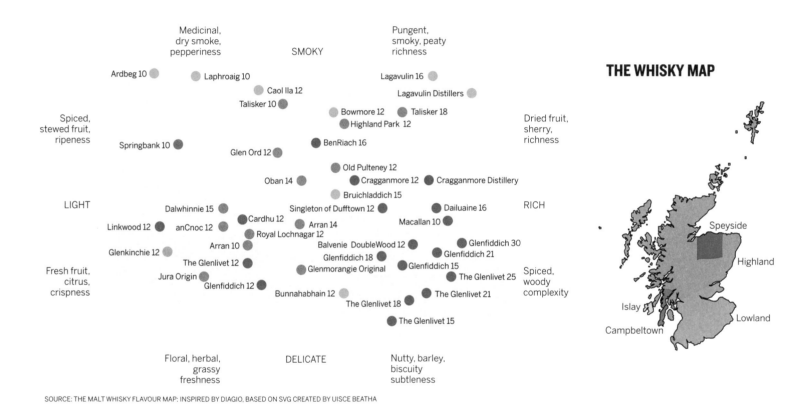

SOURCE: THE MALT WHISKY FLAVOUR MAP: INSPIRED BY DIAGIO, BASED ON SVG CREATED BY UISCE BEATHA

Although the color seems manageable, the labels are harder to sort here. When I heard *one at a time,* it turned my thoughts to small multiples—a powerful tool for reducing complexity. To use small multiples, you have to establish the structure once. I do that here with the big map. By pairing these dataviz, I can rely on using the main chart when I have time to spend with it—it's not something you can glance at and get ideas from. But the small multiples work well to highlight the regional clusters mentioned. Without much work we can see that Islay whiskys are generally very smoky, Highlands run the gamut, and Speysides are rich.

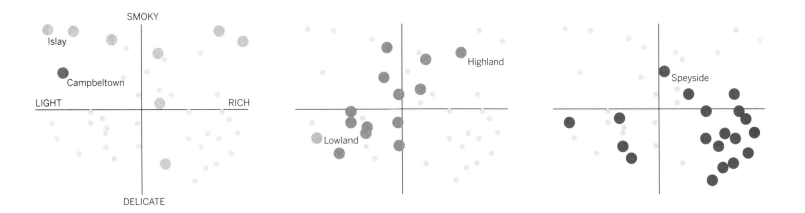

The beauty of small multiples is that once you establish the structure, you can use them on any number of variables. You could repeat the form with price, age, or whatever other variable you wanted, and several will fit into a reasonable space.

3. "Wow, the price range of whisky is all over the place. I wonder if the expensive ones have any particular flavor profile."

"What's expensive?"
"Some cost hundreds of pounds per liter. Most are clustered in the 50-to-100-pound price range, but a few are way more than that on the list I have."

"Why would some cost so much more?"
"I think it's to do with age, and probably reputation. I don't know."

"Could you add age to the mix? See whether older ones cost more?"
"I like that. Age versus price."

"Or age versus flavor profile? Do older whiskys tend to settle into a certain type of flavor?"
"Maybe I could do all three? Age, price, and flavor?"

This pushes the limits of complexity: the 2x2 includes four axes—smoky-delicate score, light-rich score, age, and price. I've used space, color, and size to encode data. That's a lot. And yet we still can look quickly and see trends and ideas. It doesn't take much work to see that expensive whiskys tend toward richness and tend to be older; the bubbles get bigger and darker as we move right. For the most part, expensive whiskys are rich and delicate.

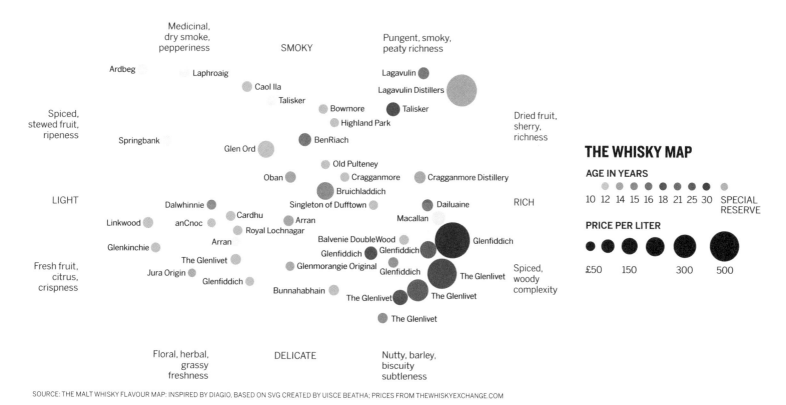

SOURCE: THE MALT WHISKY FLAVOUR MAP: INSPIRED BY DIAGIO, BASED ON SVG CREATED BY UISCE BEATHA; PRICES FROM THEWHISKYEXCHANGE.COM

Despite its complexity, this chart has that rare ability to give us an idea quickly but also allow us to spend time with it if we want to think more deeply about all that's going on here. We've lost regional information, though, and if that's important, we have to take another tack.

4. "There are a lot of interesting variables here, but I want to focus on simple comparisons."

"Why?"
"I just think in this case, for this audience, making one comparison at a time will work better. I don't want them sitting there trying to figure out three or four variables at a time during the presentation. I just want to be able to show 'this versus that' and 'that versus this' over and over."

"So, like, price versus age. Smokiness versus region. So on."
"Exactly. Nice and simple. One at a time."

It was clear from this conversation that the depth and complexity of the previous efforts—while appropriate if the audience has time to spend with the chart—would not do for this presentation. The phrase *one at a time* and the description of *this versus that* imply any number of simple two-axis charts—bars, for example, would work well here. I chose the compact dot plot—all data plotted on one horizontal axis. Comparisons within the set are easy, because you need to measure only the distance between dots, not the difference in height between bars that may not be adjacent. And these comparisons are simple: region versus richness; age versus smokiness. You could do price versus age, price versus richness, and so forth.

WHISKY AGE AND FLAVOR
Each dot represents a whisky

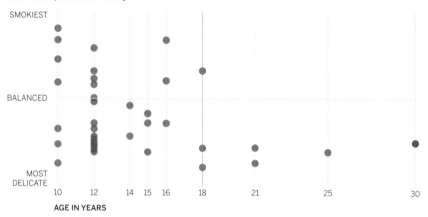

Stacking up the dot plots cleverly creates a sort of scatter plot. This is more immediately obvious on the age–smokiness chart, where we can look at whiskys of any age, or at all of them, and see that older whiskys aren't smoky.

The dot plot is a powerful way to show simple comparisons. You could create as few or as many as you wanted here. But notice that I didn't label individual points. That's a weakness. A dot plot's compactness means it isn't conducive to comprehensive labeling. If it were important to show every brand of whisky, you'd have trouble doing that here. You might try a bar chart or something else. If you wanted to label a few points of particular interest, you could probably still use a dot plot.

It's important to remember that even though this challenge started with lots of data points, it still came from just six variables, and yet I was able to stretch and twist it into several different forms and conjure still more forms I didn't plot. I'm often amazed at how much variation is possible, just as, in music, a few chords can produce an endless number of tunes.

CHAPTER 4

PRACTICING PERSUASION

"To make converts is the natural ambition of everyone."   —Goethe

GETTING SOMEONE TO *SEE* IDEAS in data is good. Getting them to *change their thinking* because of what they see is special. To move people, to bust their assumptions, to gain allies, or just to get funding, you need to persuade—not just inform—them. But persuasion isn't easy. It requires a balance of aggressiveness and restraint. You need to actively shift people's eyes and minds to where you want them to go, but you also need to refrain from rigging your charts to make that happen. The line between persuasion and unfair manipulation is blurry, and you shouldn't cross it.

At the same time, to suggest that you should avoid persuasion altogether is wrong. Passively reporting statistics with no point of view is unrealistic. In fact, it's impossible. Any chart is a manipulation—some combination of conscious and unconscious decisions about how to use space, what to include or exclude, and when to highlight or downplay. You need to make good decisions so that your charts are *positively* persuasive. Consider, for a hot-button issue such as immigration, how the exact same data can be used to create two remarkably divergent visualizations:

IMMIGRANT SHARE OF THE POPULATION APPROACHES 1910 LEVELS

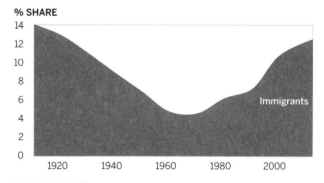

% SHARE

SOURCE: PEW RESEARCH

NON-IMMIGRANT SHARE OF THE POPULATION, 1910–2013

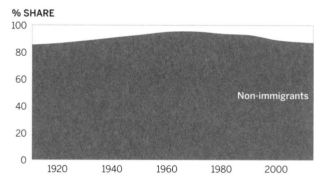

% SHARE

Follow these guidelines when trying to build persuasion into your charts.

1 **Shift your context question.** Before I make a chart, I ask myself, *What am I trying to say, to whom, and where?* This helps me produce visualizations that convey the right idea to the right people in the right format. When it comes time to be persuasive, this exercise can be amended by adding a new prompt: *I need to convince them that . . .* Compare "I'm trying to say that competitors' revenues are growing" with "I need to convince them that competitors' growing revenues are a real threat to us." The latter can lead to a different visual solution.

2 **Emphasize and isolate.** To make your visualization persuasive, shine a bright light on the most salient information. Limit the number of places an audience can focus. Move their eyes to where you want them to go. If a competitive threat will persuade them to shift strategy, emphasize that threat by making it bolder and more colorful and making everything else lighter colors or gray. The secondary information will recede, and your main point won't have to fight for attention. This advice applies to all chart making to a degree, but in persuasive viz, be blunt with it. Persuasion time is not the time for depth, nuance, and detail. Insurance companies' ads don't persuade you to buy their products by providing all their plans and prices in a structured table so that you can make an informed decision. They say, "Fifteen minutes can save you 15% or more." One idea, emphasized and isolated.

3 **Consider your reference points.** The ultimate form of isolation is to remove any information that doesn't directly support your point. If what matters is what has happened to inventory in the past three months, remove inventory data from a year ago that also appears in that spreadsheet column. Zoom in on the part that matters most. If your report always compares the performances of four regions but you really want to focus on just two of them, remove the other two. You're not persuasive if you provide the audience a chart that invites multiple interpretations, and the more data you include, the more likely they will find alternative interpretations.

Conversely, think beyond your data set to what you might add to the chart to increase its persuasive power. New and different points of comparison can make an audience see something familiar in a fresh way. A report on productivity that usually shows hours lost might instead visualize FTE positions that could be filled if the cost of that time were recouped. New reference points can shift their thinking from *how many* hours have been lost to the *value* of lost hours.

4 **Point things out.** It doesn't take much to move someone's eyes. Pointers, demarcations, and simple labels signal to an audience what matters. Highlighting a section of a scatter plot makes it clear that this is the "active zone." Point an arrow to a gap in the data and label it "the opportunity." That's explicit. The gap itself draws viewers' eyes; the label tells the audience what to think about it. You could add a "danger" line (probably red) to a line chart. If the trend sinks below that line, it's time to panic. We see a trend in relation to an idea. It makes us think about what it means to cross a line.

5 **Lure.** Upending expectations can be powerfully persuasive. If you set up your chart with a visual the audience expects to see and then show how reality differs from their expectations, you create a moment of psychological tension. It forces them to reconcile the disconnect—why what they thought was true is not. Evidence to the contrary is challenging and will foster discussion: Here's what you think our data looks like; here's how it actually looks. This approach works well to delight and engage the audience in presentations.

6 **Bonus pro tip: Use narrative structure.** Nothing is as persuasive, as uniquely human, as a story. It's the most effective form of communication we have. People don't just respond to narrative; they crave it. So tell stories with your charts. "Storytelling with data" is a phrase that's starting to show signs of wear. Many people talk about doing it, but often they have no idea what it really means. All I mean by it is that you can benefit from using the basic structure of a story to create a chart or a series of charts. That structure is:

- *Setup*: Let me show you some reality.
- *Conflict*: Here is something that happened to that reality.
- *Resolution*: Here is the new reality after the conflict.

In most stories, conflict or "rising action" is adversarial. A storm, a duel, or a married person's unexpected love interest. With charts, we're liberally interpreting the term "conflict." It's often adversarial but sometimes it's just a change, or even a positive change. A big new client was acquired, or a promotion was won. Data sets involving a time element (sign-ups by quarter, or REM sleep during the night) lend themselves to storytelling, but others will work in this structure as well.

The following challenges are designed to develop skills in persuasiveness. Focus on ways to increase the persuasive power of your ideas without being dishonestly manipulative. For these challenges don't worry about alternate forms, or color choices, or other considerations, unless they help persuade.

PRACTICING PERSUASION WARM-UP

1. Which of the following statements is a good contextual starting point for developing a persuasive chart?

   A "I need to show them our declining overseas revenue."

   B "I want them to see the two-year revenue trend in every market so that they can see that revenues are declining more in most of the 13 overseas markets than they are in our home markets—and by percentages higher than seasonal or historical averages."

   C "I need to prove to them that the revenue trend overseas is troubling. Especially in the past six months."

2. This chart convincingly shows a precipitous drop in employee vacation days taken. Identify two ways in which it may be unfairly manipulative.

THE ABRUPT FALL OF THE AMERICAN VACATION

AVERAGE ANNUAL VACATION DAYS USED

% FULL-WEEK VACATIONS

SOURCE: OXFORD ECONOMICS ANALYSIS, BASED ON A GFK PUBLIC AFFAIRS AND COMMUNICATION SURVEY AND DATA BY U.S. BUREAU OF LABOR STATISTICS, ON BEHALF OF "PROJECT: TIME OFF" (2014)

3. You want to convince your boss that marketing should focus on fewer product features when offering a new credit card. Your analysis tells you that only the top three features offered drive meaningful conversion. Sketch a way to make a more persuasive case.

WHAT DO CUSTOMERS WANT FROM THEIR CREDIT CARDS?

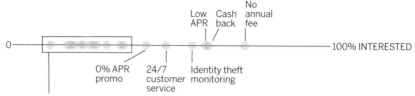

(In descending order of interest)
Retailer rewards
Entry period bonus incentive
Transferable points
Restaurant rewards
No foreign transaction fees
Airline miles/travel rewards
Hotel rewards
Comprehensive mobile app
Online chat support
Contactless payment
Access to events
Concierge service

SOURCE: COMPANY RESEARCH

4. New context for the above chart: Your bosses are convinced that retail rewards and a mobile app are what will drive credit card purchases. Sketch out a presentation of the data that will persuade them that's not the case and that you think they should stick to the basics.

5. Your scatter plot shows the weight (x-axis), height (y-axis) and speed (dot color) of hundreds of American football players. You want to convince your audience that American football players are uniquely massive and powerful. List some of the ways you could alter your scatter plot, adding and removing reference points to make this point clearer and more persuasive.

6. You've amassed data on noise-pollution levels from a street corner over the course of a year. List some reference points not included in your data that you could add to help persuade people that the noise level on this corner is unacceptable.

7. You want to show your team that there's an opportunity to increase traffic to your website between 12:25 p.m. and 2:10 p.m. Adjust this chart to make it more persuasive on that point.

THE LUNCHTIME TRAFFIC DIP

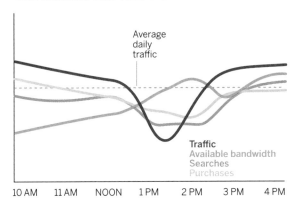

8. Which of the following statements will most likely lead to a chart that veers into unfair manipulation?

A "I need to convince them that they've set the year-end goals way too high, that there's no historical precedent for such aggressive targets, and that we're being set up for failure."

B "I have to show them how ridiculous they're being and that they're doing this just to make us look bad. The year-end goal is so off the charts that we'll basically fail by the end of the first quarter. There's no chance for success, and they need to stop being idiots."

C "I want to show them how unlikely it is that we can attain the goals they've set for the year."

9. The scatter plot here shows a reasonably linear correlation between price and download speed. But the line chart shows that download speed is not a linear function. How might you adjust the scatter plot to amplify the point that our sense of the value of the bandwidth we pay for is skewed?

THE PRICE OF SPEED

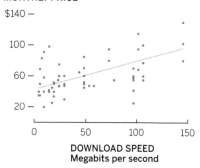

MONTHLY PRICE

SOURCE: STEFANO PUNTONI

THE TIME BENEFIT OF SPEED

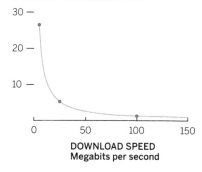

MINUTES TO DOWNLOAD 1 GB

10. Tell a story with this chart. Write out a setup, a conflict, and a resolution and then sketch how you could present each part of the story.

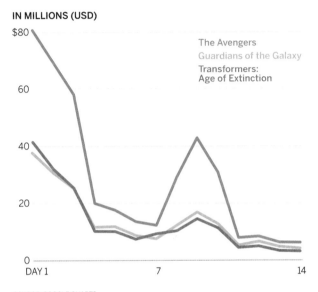

BOX OFFICE EARNINGS, FIRST TWO WEEKS

IN MILLIONS (USD)

The Avengers
Guardians of the Galaxy
Transformers:
Age of Extinction

SOURCE: GOOGLE CHARTS

DISCUSSION

1. Answer: C. This statement is imperative and focused. Option A is too passive and general. The speaker just wants to show people something. There's no analysis or persuasive impulse in the statement. He may be thinking that it's a troubling trend, but because he hasn't explicitly said so, it's unlikely his chart will reflect that sense of trouble. Option B is so laden with detail that it could become two or three charts. The statement has no clear point of focus and, again, no persuasive idea. The speaker is describing data, not an idea she wants viewers to grasp. With option C you can almost see a persuasive chart: One line for overseas revenue over the past six months, with domestic revenue as a gray secondary line or another line showing historical trends.

2. 1. *Width.* The narrower the chart, the steeper the hills. Sometimes the space is what you have or what you need to use. Imagine, for example, that another chart will sit beside this one on the page. But in a typical presentation, or on a typical screen or piece of paper, there's room to make time series horizontal. When the chart is widened, the trend is still falling, but it looks less abrupt: this decline takes time.

THE ABRUPT FALL OF THE AMERICAN VACATION

AVERAGE ANNUAL VACATION DAYS USED — % FULL-WEEK VACATIONS

SOURCE: OXFORD ECONOMICS ANALYSIS, BASED ON A GFK PUBLIC AFFAIRS AND COMMUNICATION SURVEY AND DATA BY U.S. BUREAU OF LABOR STATISTICS, ON BEHALF OF "PROJECT: TIME OFF" (2014)

2. *Truncated y-axes.* Another way to make curves steeper is to truncate values from the y-axes. Fewer values means more distance between them. Here I've limited the y-axis range to the high and low values in the data—a common approach. Sometimes that's okay. (Scientific values clustered together between, say, 1 and 1.1 may not benefit from a full y-axis that would tightly cluster all the values in a small part of the chart area. Differences in

values that are meaningful may be hidden or hard to see because of the full y-axis.) Here we're dealing with vacation days, whether that means one or 21. And the percentage of full-week vacations should start at 0. Truncating here effectively means hiding data. This chart certainly highlights the decline, but is it fair to make it this steep? Look at the same data without truncated axes: at the very least, the decline appears less abrupt.

THE ABRUPT FALL OF THE AMERICAN VACATION

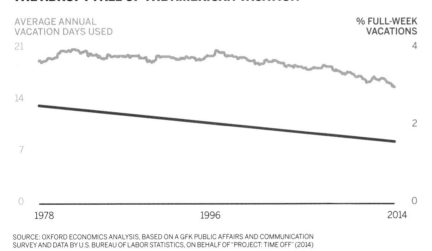

SOURCE: OXFORD ECONOMICS ANALYSIS, BASED ON A GFK PUBLIC AFFAIRS AND COMMUNICATION SURVEY AND DATA BY U.S. BUREAU OF LABOR STATISTICS, ON BEHALF OF "PROJECT: TIME OFF" (2014)

3. My approach involved removing most of the information from the chart and adding just a couple of key markers. The original encourages me to read and compare everything. I want to know what all those features are and where they fall on the interest scale. Even if I treat that block of features as one variable, I'm left with seven variables to compare (the top six and the rest).

But the challenge is to persuade the bosses that the company should focus on fewer product features. One easy way to do that is to literally remove things they *could* focus on so that their eyes go where you want them to. Label only the good features, and all the rest become just "do not convert." The dividing line makes the idea even more explicit.

FEW FEATURES
DRIVE ACCOUNT CREATION

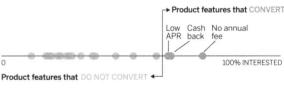

SOURCE: COMPANY RESEARCH

A note of caution: If you use this kind of persuasion, you had better be able to defend your analysis. Can you explain why and how the top three convert and the others don't? If not, you're making arbitrary distinctions that feel unfairly manipulative. And be prepared to talk about the variables you haven't labeled, because you may very well get questions about them—What are they? If you had to pick one to explore further, which would it be? In short, know your stuff.

4. Here's an excellent opportunity to use a *lure procedure*: psychologists' term for a bait and switch. Here the bait is what the bosses expect. They believe the new features are working, but your analysis demonstrates that they are not. By showing them their expectations first and reality next, you create a moment of surprise and a need to reconcile the disparity. Their brains want to understand why what they thought was true isn't. It's a compelling way to help someone see something in a new way. If this were being presented on paper or in a small setting, the "expected" and "actual" charts would probably suffice.

I've created three charts for a presentation setting. Here's a script to accompany them:

1. "As you know, we surveyed customers about their interest in all the features of our credit cards, and they found some more interesting than others."

WHAT DRIVES CONSUMERS TO GET A CREDIT CARD

0   100% INTERESTED

2. "We invested in adding retail rewards and the app, thinking customers would really want those new features. So, were those features the ones that scored highest?"
(Pause)

WE EXPECTED NEW FEATURES TO DRIVE CONVERSION

New feature, such as retail rewards and mobile app

Existing feature, such as no annual fee and cash back

EXPECTED RESULTS

0   100% INTERESTED

3. "No. The basic features we've offered for years are still the ones customers are most interested in. In fact, our analysis says those top three are the only ones that sway potential customers to adopt our product."

BUT THE BASICS STILL DRIVE ACCOUNT CREATION

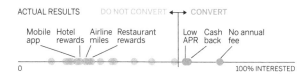

ACTUAL RESULTS   DO NOT CONVERT ←→ CONVERT

Mobile   Hotel   Airline Restaurant   Low   Cash   No annual
app   rewards miles   rewards   APR   back   fee

0   100% INTERESTED

5. Here's a fun exercise for really messing with reference points. In my mind's eye, I saw a scatter plot with players getting taller, heavier, and slower in lockstep. I prototyped it:

BIG AND FAST

American football players are not like us.

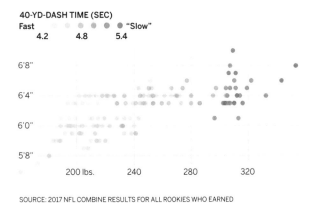

SOURCE: 2017 NFL COMBINE RESULTS FOR ALL ROOKIES WHO EARNED
A SPOT ON AN NFL ROSTER; PRO-FOOTBALL-FOCUS.COM

From this I could see that these guys are big and fast. I could also see the general correlation between size and speed. But to make immediately accessible the idea that these people are uniquely massive and powerful, I needed to add some reference points—such as a person who's not a football player—for comparison. I could use any number of them: other athletes, historical figures, animals, even myself. In this case I chose two:

BIG AND FAST

American football players are not like us.

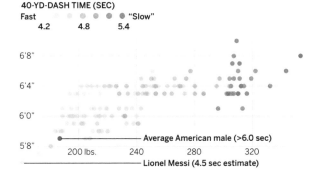

SOURCE: 2017 NFL COMBINE RESULTS FOR ALL ROOKIES WHO EARNED
A SPOT ON AN NFL ROSTER; PRO-FOOTBALL-FOCUS.COM

Seeing another world-class athlete barely make it onto the chart puts the size of American football players into a new, convincing perspective. I deliberately put Messi "off the chart" to suggest that we're dealing here with another category of size altogether. Putting the average, hopelessly slow American male near the bottom accomplishes the same. But this is still a lot of data, and our focus still goes to the player dots. We're tempted to spend more time with them than with the comparison. One way to make the comparison more immediate is to remove reference points and use the average size of players by position:

BIG AND FAST

If you're an average American male, you're smaller than the average small defensive back and slower than the average offensive lineman.

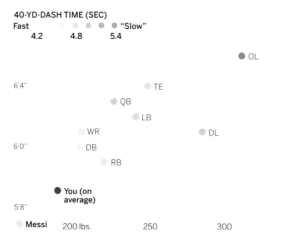

40-YD-DASH TIME (SEC)

COULD YOU BEAT AN OFFENSIVE LINEMAN IN A FOOTRACE?

No, you couldn't.

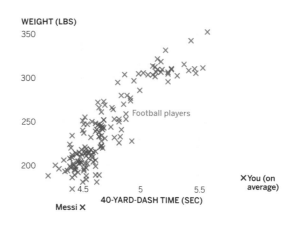

Using "you" for average is playful and would work if the audience were mostly average American men, but in general the average-person data point should probably be labeled more clearly. This view of the idea is somewhat persuasive too, but encoding speed in color isn't ideal for conveying the sense of size combined with power. Big people shouldn't be able to run as fast as most pro football players can. One way to highlight speed better would be to remove height from the visualization. Height is interesting, but speed is more interesting. We could make the trade-off, forgoing height and putting speed on a spatial axis rather than a color one:

This is playful. When that's appropriate, it can enhance engagement and a chart's persuasiveness. But know your audience. If they don't want to joke around, refrain. I used crosses here just to see how they might read compared with dots. I do that sometimes to test design ideas. In this case I think it's fine, because I'm not trying to get you to see anything in the red other than the overall cluster. We don't need to discern positions or individual data points. I could just as well have left the dots. The decision to remove weight is the focus here; you commonly have enough good material to get to a good chart in multiple ways. Often there's no right answer—it may come down to simple preference. Here I could make a case for either the three-variable plot with height, weight, and color or the one that removes height. I could use dots or crosses. The broader point is that I'm persuasively manipulating reference points.

6. Using information outside your data set is an important and underutilized tactic for making charts persuasive. The subtle semantic shift from visualizing data to visualizing an idea can open you to the notion that the idea can be crafted using more than just data. Here are some common, consistently useful outside reference points:

   - *Historical precedent.* How does your data compare with a similar set from the past? Example: Voter turnout in this election compared with turnout in past elections.
   - *Competitive set.* What does your visual look like when compared with some competitive force? Example: the accuracy of your algorithm versus that of similar algorithms.
   - *Regrouping.* What does your data look like if you group variables differently? Example: Sales team performance by region regrouped as sales team performance by product sold.
   - *Statistical patterns.* How does your data compare with what we'd expect to see

statistically? Example: Actual distribution of student grades versus expected distribution.
   - *Unexpected reference points.* What does your data look like compared with something completely unrelated or creative that the audience can identify with? Example: Miles traveled by delivery staffers compared with how many times they've traveled the same distance as to the moon.

For the noisy street corner challenge, I conjured a few reference points that might make the data come alive:

- Data from another corner or several other corners added to show how loud this one is relative to others (competitive set).
- A comparison of the average noise level, the peak noise level, and the lowest noise level with other sounds, such as animals, jet engines, rushing water, or a library (unexpected comparisons).
- Average noise mapped against a distribution of average urban noise levels to see whether the noise here is typical or an outlier (statistical patterns).
- Stress levels plotted against noise levels to show how the sound affects anxiety (unexpected comparisons).

7. Sometimes the most persuasive charts are the simplest; they present one idea so unmistakably clearly that the audience has nothing else to focus on or no other way to interpret what they see. Given the very specific context provided here, we can remove almost all the data in this chart except the opportunity. The other data may be interesting for other contexts—How does bandwidth rise and fall with traffic? Does more traffic translate to more purchases? But those weren't the context. I can visualize what's needed with very few elements. I don't even use values on the y-axis, and I've put only the bounds of the opportunity on the x-axis, in case there's any doubt about what's important. No words are needed to see where the opportunity is here. (It was a happy accident that the word *Opportunity* in the headline falls right above the opportunity in the chart.)

8. Answer: B. This speaker is certainly passionate, but notice the focus on the attitude of the audience (they're "idiots" being "ridiculous") and on ideas that don't come from the data. "There's no chance for success" may be true, but it's not something you can visualize. This person wants to pick a fight, not persuade—so it's easy to imagine that emotion will lead the chart into manipulative territory. The chart maker may ignore important variables or visuals that soften the case as a way of avoiding hard truths. Option C feels passive and general, but it appears to be leading not so much to trouble as to a chart that's insufficiently persuasive. Option A looks promising. It is focused on data (goals are too high, and *historical precedents* for targets can be plotted) and feels active and passionate without being angry.

THE LUNCHTIME TRAFFIC OPPORTUNITY

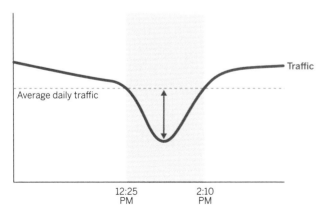

9. The original charts tell an important story: We pay double for double bandwidth, but we don't get double the performance! Once we understand that the most value comes by increasing from 0 to 50 megabits per second, and that the value increase diminishes significantly after that, we can make some judgments about the cost–speed relationship. In this case I want to show that viewers may think paying a moderate price for extremely high speeds is "a deal," but it's not nearly as good a deal as they think. Meanwhile, paying more to get from, say, 10 to 25 Mbps is a much better value than they think. The biggest rip-offs are the very-high-bandwidth offers that cost the most. As the chart shows, people are paying a lot for small, incremental gains. Creating zones (and using "cool" colors for value and "hot" colors for little value) creates a more immediate association between cost and value than the previous chart provides. Of course, you have to be able to defend these value judgments.

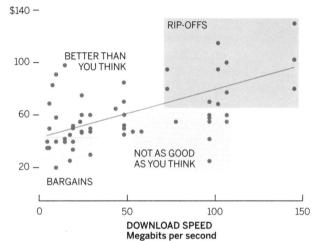

THE PRICE OF SPEED

MONTHLY PRICE

SOURCE: STEFANO PUNTONI

10. Time series charts lend themselves well to storytelling techniques. To make them into a story you can selectively reveal the x-axis, as I've done here. Here's the story in the form of presentation notes. The narrative frame is highlighted:

THE AVENGERS WEEK I: STRONG BUT TYPICAL

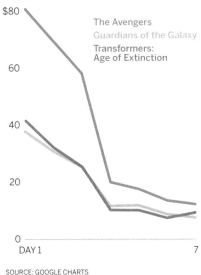

BOX OFFICE IN MILLIONS (USD)

SOURCE: GOOGLE CHARTS

Setup: *The Avengers* opening was a massive success, dwarfing the box-office performance of other superhero movies. But the pattern it followed over the next week was similar to that of other movies in the genre, albeit at a higher level: a big opening that declines over the weekend and tapers off during the week.

THE AVENGERS SECOND WEEKEND: NOT AT ALL TYPICAL

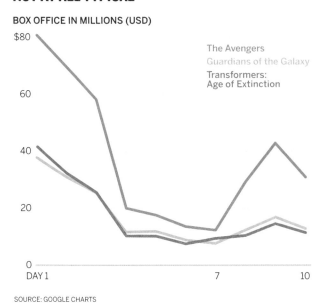

BOX OFFICE IN MILLIONS (USD)

SOURCE: GOOGLE CHARTS

Conflict: Usually the second weekend shows a modest bump in box-office receipts, but *The Avengers* surprisingly had a huge bump. It grossed as much in its second weekend as most superhero flicks haul in on their opening weekend.

THE AVENGERS WEEK 2: BACK TO NORMAL

BOX OFFICE IN MILLIONS (USD)

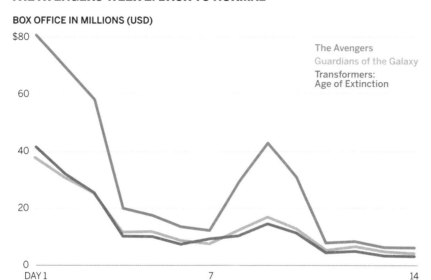

The Avengers
Guardians of the Galaxy
Transformers:
Age of Extinction

SOURCE: GOOGLE CHARTS

Resolution: During week two *The Avengers* finally settled into the normal pattern, matching the performance of other superhero movies.

ELAN INC. OVERTAKES POMME CO.

POMME SHARE PRICE (USD)

ELAN SHARE PRICE (USD)

GIVING GOOD STOCK ADVICE

The more you learn about making good charts, the more you'll notice abuses of persuasive techniques—some deliberate, most accidental—that unfairly manipulate reality. This simple view of stock prices over 11 months is just such an animal. At first blush it looks good and tells a clean story, reflected in the headline. It's clear and well designed. It even looks official. Unfortunately, it's grossly manipulative. As you gain dataviz literacy, you'll want to be able to identify how a chart like this tries to put one over on viewers and how to change it to more responsibly reflect the truth. Let's work on it.

1. Find and explain three ways this chart unfairly manipulates the user.
2. Sketch a version of it using share price that better reflects reality.
3. Sketch an alternative chart that supports the idea that Elan Inc. is the stronger investment.

(sketch space)

DISCUSSION

This chart is irresistible. We immediately see a compelling story whose crisp, declarative headline couldn't be more succinct. There it is in pink and blue: Elan Inc.'s stock shot past Pomme Co.'s. But a closer look reveals the false narrative. Even if it takes only a few seconds to recognize the game, it's still hard to unsee the narrative. Compelling charts have a high *facticity*—a term researchers use to describe the feeling that something is objectively true. Our minds love to find a story in the picture; they want to believe what they see, and it takes effort to understand what's really going on without recharting.

1. 1. *The dual y-axis uses the same variable in different ranges.* Elan's value tops out at $200, but it's at the same height as Pomme's $1,000. So at the point where the two share prices "cross," Elan's value is actually one-fifth Pomme's. Once Elan's line rises above Pomme's, we see its share price as higher, but it's not.

   Dual y-axes in general make charts difficult to use. Measuring two different things in the same space is like playing chess and backgammon on the same board at the same time.

   2. *The headline.* The word *overtakes* in the headline reinforces the rising pink line. The chart maker has made it too easy to glance at the lines, see the headline, and form the false narrative. In general, headlines are good for reinforcing ideas, but if they're reinforcing false ideas that's an unfair manipulation.

   3. *The semi-logarithmic scale.* This point is subtler. Did you notice that the y-axis lines aren't equidistant? This chart is known as "log-linear," because the y-axis is plotted logarithmically, and the x-axis is linear. A log scale shows equal distance between exponents, so low-end values will be further apart than high-end ones. Log scales are usually used to plot large ranges of values, or when outliers are so far away from most values that a majority of the plots are in a corner, squashed so close together that you can't see any patterns. If, for example, most of your data fits into the 10-to-100 range but five values are in the 10,000 range, it would be hard to see any

difference between most of your values on a linear scale. The log scale stretches out the low end so that you can see differences but also plot outliers or higher values.

Statisticians and scientists are accustomed to log scales, but most of us find them hard to readily grasp. I struggle with them. Charles Richter, inventor of the logarithmic Richter scale for measuring earthquake intensity, is known to have said, "Logarithmic plots are a device of the devil." You should probably use them only when necessary and when you know your audience will understand them.

Here the log scale is completely unnecessary—even illogical. The ranges aren't stretched such that they demand exponential treatment. Even more pernicious is that because log scales stretch the low values and squish the high values, this chart exaggerates Elan's rise, which happens mostly on the low end.

2. The easiest fix here is a single, linear y-axis in the range of all stock price values from $0 to about $700—close enough in value to warrant a linear range. Suddenly the word *overtakes* is at odds with what we see. I've changed the headline because I still want to persuade people that Elan is the stronger investment. But despite the headline, you might think from this chart that Elan's performance is unimpressive. Although Elan outperformed Pomme in this period, it's hard to get that feeling from this chart. It doesn't persuade me of Elan's strength. To make the point persuasive, I need to find another way to express the data.

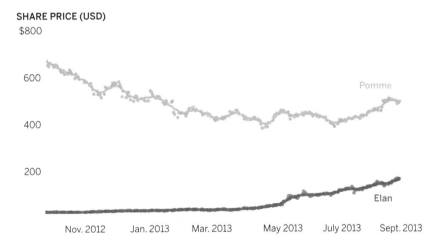

ELAN INC. STRONGER THAN POMME CO.

SHARE PRICE (USD)

3. Investments are more about volatility and change in value than about raw value. We care less how much it costs than how the cost compares with what we paid. To see that, make what we paid a 0 point and then plot the percentage change in that value over time. The same initial data will produce a radically different view—and one that's far more persuasive about the value of investing in Elan versus Pomme.

In some cases you may need both charts. If the audience for this visualization doesn't know that despite Pomme's flat performance, one of its shares is worth five times as much as an Elan share, they should be told.

ELAN INC. RISING, POMME CO. EBBING

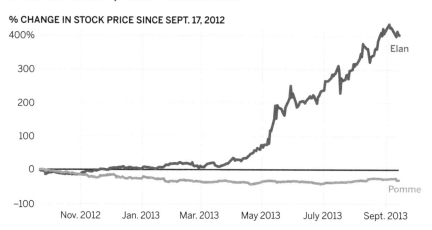

% CHANGE IN STOCK PRICE SINCE SEPT. 17, 2012

PERSUADING A PATIENT TO GET SOME SLEEP

Health care providers want to help patients make good decisions. That's not easy. Health data isn't always easy to understand, and at highly stressful moments, such as immediately after a difficult diagnosis, patients can hardly even think straight, much less make decisions about their care. Data visualization can help—and more generally, it can be the persuasive element that turns a dense set of data about the body's workings into a decision-making tool. Here is a doctor's report on a patient's test for symptoms of sleep apnea. The doctor knows that this patient is skeptical of the diagnosis; he must convince the patient that his symptoms have entered the "moderate" stage and should be treated. He has even highlighted some of the most important data, but the patient is unpersuaded. Let's work on it.

1. List three things about the table that could be improved to make them more effective for a patient.
2. Sketch a version of this data as a visual report. Don't focus on getting the data just right. Focus on creating forms you might use for the various elements in the report.
3. Given the baseline data in the two severity indexes in the bottom right of the table, make some sketches based on the report that will persuade the patient to address his sleep apnea.

Patient Name: **VAN WINKLE, RIP**	Study Date: 8/14/17
Gender: M	Patient ID #: 95030
Birth Date: 9/6/72	Patient Age: 45 years
Height: 71 inches	Weight: 220
Referring: P. Vanderdonk, MD	Interpreting: W. Irving, MD

Events	#/hour	Total	Mean duration (sec)	Max duration (sec)
Central Apneas	4.1	30	15.3	19.0
Obstructive Apneas	6.8	49	19.4	41.0
Hypopneas	11.5	83	22.2	45.5
Apneas + Hypopneas	22.4	162	20.7	45.5

Snoring	
Total Snoring Episodes	59
Total Duration Snoring	15.7 min
Mean Duration Snoring	16.0 sec
Percentage of Snoring	3.6%

Time of Study	
Lights Off	11:38 PM
Lights On	6:53 AM
Monitoring Time	435 min

Oximetry Distribution	Duration (min)	% of time
<100%	30	7
<95%	290	67
<90%	32	7
<85%	25	6
<80%	28	6
<75%	20	5
<70%	10	2

Apnea + Hypopnea Severity Index	
Minimal	<5 events/hour
Mild	5 - 15 events/hour
Moderate	15 - 30 events/hour
Severe	>30 events/hour

Heart Rate	BPM
Mean HR during sleep:	54
Highest HR during sleep:	95
Lowest HR during sleep:	48

Oxygen Desaturation	
Average (%)	88
Total # of Desats	85
Desat Index (#/hour)	11.8
Desat Max (%)	28
Desat Max dur (sec)	48
Low SpO$_2$%	78
Duration of Low SpO$_2$%	5

Oximetry Desaturation Severity Index	
Normal	>95%
Mild	90–95%
Moderate	80–89%
Severe	<80%

(sketch space)

DISCUSSION

Reports like this are typical, and not just in health care. This is a classic data dump of key performance indicators. Everything we need is here, but that doesn't mean we know how to read and interpret it. And persuasion is nearly nonexistent. The highlights are a half-hearted attempt to get me to focus on parts of the report, but I'm unlikely to be convinced there's a problem, much less to take action. More needs to be done.

1. 1. *Translation of technical terms.* Doctors can use these tables; patients can't. Context: The doctor wants to persuade the patient to address his health. Terms such as *oximetry distribution* and *desat index* are going to undermine that as the patient struggles to learn what everything means before even beginning to wonder what the measurements in these categories indicate. "Total amount of oxygen in the blood" and "Number of times blood oxygen levels fell" are clearer for the audience.

   2. *Specificity.* Whether the mean duration of a hypopnea was 22.2 seconds or 22.5 seconds doesn't matter to the patient (however much it may matter to the doctor), and using decimal points when rounded numbers would do makes it harder to read.

   3. *Lack of benchmarks.* Even if the patient goes directly to the highlighted data and sees what the doctor wants him to see, he's almost certainly going to ask, *Is that normal?* This report provides numbers without any value judgment, when that's what matters most. Are the numbers good? Acceptable? Poor? Dire? The patient needs reference points to show how this information stacks up against what the doctor expects or wants.

You might wonder why I'm critiquing the table rather than heading straight into chart making. Two reasons. First, critiquing the presentation of data sets you up to make better charts, because you'll have seen what's missing and what's difficult to understand. Second, in many cases you want to provide a table like this after the audience has seen a visual so that they can take a deeper dive—so it helps to ensure that you can create good tables as well.

2. Effectively, this challenge is to build a small dashboard for sleep performance. My effort is just a start and leaves plenty of room for improvement. I stopped here to show the work in progress—how I systematically moved through the various tables looking for simple ways to visualize. I should note that these sketches represent the second or third (albeit rapid) iterations of the ideas. Let's discuss them from left to right, top to bottom.

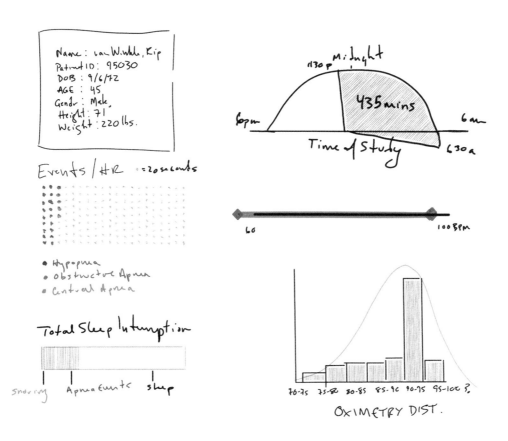

Basic patient data: table. I saw no need to visualize this information. It's core data that works fine as a table.

Time of study: arc. I used the notion of a 24-hour clock to show both how long the study lasted (shaded area) and in what time span it occurred (horizontal axis). I haven't yet decided how to divvy up the time, but I put midnight at the top because in the mind's eye that's where midnight is. On the other hand, 6 p.m. appears where we expect to see 9 p.m. and 6 a.m. where we expect to see 3 a.m. So I also toyed with using a full circle here. If daytime were involved in the sleep issue, it would be easy to add sunrise and sunset markers here as well. I wanted to work on this more. This visual could be very small. It communicates simple, basic information.

Events/hour: unit chart. A sleep apnea event is a short period during which a person stops breathing or struggles to breathe. In most cases sufferers have dozens to hundreds of these a night, a manageable number for showing each event as its own visual mark—in this case a dot. Marking individual units on a visualization always helps the audience see those events as more than a collection of statistics formulated into something abstract, such as a bar. Apnea is an event, and each dot here represents an event. I can categorize units of time with colors to represent the type of event that occurred. Adding units for "good sleep" time helps paint the big picture for the patient: Here's when you were breathing, and here's when you weren't. Well-organized unit charts have the effect of simultaneously being powerful displays of individual units and more-holistic stacked bar charts, like this one. Units are inherently reusable, too. If you know when each event happened, you can redeploy the colored dots on a histogram to show when the patient stopped breathing.

Heart rate: lollipop chart. So named because the dot-and-line combo looks something like the candy, these charts are a great, simple way to show ranges or distance between two points. This one shows the range of heart rates over the course of the night. Adding a scale from 60 to 100—the typical range for human heartbeats—provides a reference. My only hesitation here was that the average BPM while the patient slept was 54, meaning that for the most part the heart rate was below the scale and the rate spiked only a few times to a higher rate. This visual may over-emphasize those short bursts by showing the range without any distribution of frequency. A histogram would show that more immediately. I've made a trade-off here.

Total sleep interruption: stacked bar. I felt that the data set included similar information in different places. Snoring was separate from apnea events, but both interrupt sleep. Adding those two things together allows us to compare wakeful time with sleeping time. The amount of wakeful time in that bar is somewhat astonishing: nearly 30 minutes out of 435. One caveat: It's unclear whether the snoring and apnea overlapped, so I'd have to confirm that they were separate events before presenting this way.

Oximetry distribution: histogram. The word *distribution* sent me right to the most common chart type for that—a histogram. Oximetry measures how much oxygen is in the blood, and more is better, so this chart should skew right. Histograms look like bar charts, though traditionally their bars touch. Someone without experience using one may mistake it for a bar chart and not immediately understand how to read it. It sometimes helps to provide prototypical distributions (average, good, bad) for comparison, or to explain in words, as I just did, how you want this visual to look.

If this were to become something I wanted to give to patients, my next step would be to think about creating some hierarchy of information. I wouldn't keep all the visual elements the same size, and I'd fiddle with the order of what's presented. I'd want to create a dominant visual and some supporting ones, and I'd want to make sure the ideas progressed logically.

If you're so inclined, a great exercise is to take your sketches to the next level: Imagine you will be handing this piece of paper to a patient. How would you design it?

3. Now I'm actively trying to persuade a patient to change his behavior. The dashboard exercise created a more engaging entry into a lot of data, which may help patients get beyond a page full of numbers, but it didn't do much more than present findings dispassionately. Changing behavior is difficult and requires more-aggressive tactics. My attempts at persuasion here focus on two main elements. First, I address the

patient directly whenever I can: This is not just data, it's *your* data. This is when *you* stop breathing. Poor results become something the patient owns. Second, I added some qualitative ranges and labels. Even good charts that get to meaning quickly may lack useful parameters. You'll hear reactions such as *So is this good? Is this normal? Where should I be on here?* By emphasizing good and bad results (and using green for the former and red for the latter), I help the patient see not only what his results are but also what they mean.

OXYGEN DESATURATION

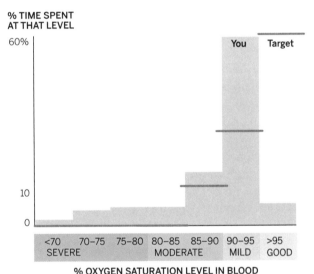

APNEA AND HYPOPNEA PER HOUR

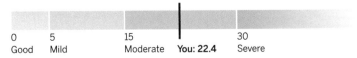

DURATION WITHOUT BREATHING

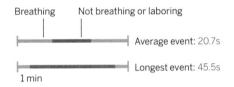

YOUR TYPICAL HOUR

Let's take these one by one with some additional commentary.

Oxygen desaturation: histogram. Even a patient unused to reading histograms will be able to use this chart. Without effort, you can see where the patient's results are above or below what they should be. To help convey the idea of distribution of frequency, I've made the axis labels a bit wordier and plainly descriptive. I toyed with making the bars in the histogram the same color as their qualitative level (green, aqua, orange, pink), or making each range's color rise up the y-axis, but all that felt overwhelming and confusing, so I opted to color code just the labels.

Apnea + hypopnea per hour: stacked bar and gauge. Here I present only one data point from the results, but we can see the power of putting that one result in the context of what's a good or a bad result. It's important to think about reference points and not assume that the best visualizations encompass the most data. I can imagine that in cases where multiple tests are done, each test could be plotted to show the general direction of results as well.

Duration without breathing: timeline. Here's another simple view that should persuade the patient to address his condition. I've plotted only two data points, an average and a maximum. But seeing the proportion of time spent not breathing is much more powerful than seeing a simple report of apnea-event lengths. I can imagine a minute; thinking about barely breathing for that amount of time is effectively frightening.

Your typical hour: timeline. In this case I used the data to create something that isn't real but represents an average hour. If I had the real data for an hour, or for a whole night, I would plot that; this timeline is representative in terms of number of events per hour and average length of event. It's a variation on the one-minute timeline, which shows only a single event—in that case we want to understand what an event is like. Here I wanted to give a sense of what events do to the patient's sleep over a longer period. It's hard not to see just how disruptive this person's moderate sleep apnea has become.

MAKING A CASE TO HR

You've sat through this presentation before, right? The important topic with plenty of data that turns into an exercise in squinting to read bullet points or ignoring the presentation while you read the paper version sitting in front of you, taking notes on it and prepping your questions—which the presenter may already have answered, but you wouldn't know, because you're not listening.

Presentation software tends to encourage this kind of disaster. The default prompts you to enter a headline and bullet points. Worse, though, the software discourages good visualization by making it easy to automatically import click-and-viz output from a spreadsheet or a table from a text document.

A good presentation should be inherently visual. The right combination of what the audience sees and what you say will make the best experience. No one should be reading while you're talking.

In this case the presenter wants to persuade the HR department to improve family leave policies for new parents. The presentation teems with good data and persuasive ideas. Good charts would transform the experience and make the case much more persuasive. Let's work on it.

I'll keep this simple with just one challenge: Transform this presentation into a persuasive one.

1 Paid parental leave at our firm versus others

- In a data set of roughly 50 firms—a mix of our industry and several adjacent industries—the average maternity leave policy was **16 weeks fully paid,** beginning sometime in the first year of employment.

- In the same data set the average paternity leave policy was **6–7 weeks fully paid.**

- Median leave was 15 weeks and 6 weeks, respectively. Mode was 16 and 6.

- In a comparison of 21 firms in our industry, our leave was shortest, at 1 week with full pay and 8 weeks with partial pay for maternity and 1 week for paternity. The best company offered 20 weeks for maternity and 12 weeks for paternity.

2 Paid parental leave at our firm versus industry competitors

BEST	Co. A	Co. B	Co. C	Co. D	Co. E
Maternity	20	16	18	16	12
Paternity	12	10	6	8	12

GOOD	Co. F	Co. G	Co. H	Co. I	Co. J	Co. K	Co. L	Co. M	Co. N	Co. O	Co. P	Co. Q
Maternity	18	12	12	8	12	6	12	12	12	12	12	12
Paternity	-	6	4	8	3	6	-	-	-	-	-	-

LAGGING	Co. R	Co. S	Co. T	Co. U	Our firm
Maternity	10	9	8	2	1
Paternity	-	1	2	2	1

3 Paid parental leave is increasingly important for recruiting young top talent

- 85% of U.S. Millennials say they're less likely to quit a company if paid parental leave is offered. (E&Y survey)

- 80% of Millennials say the top reason they stay in a job is competitive pay and benefits. (E&Y survey)

- Paid leave is not merely a women's issue for this generation: 78% of Millennials are part of a two-career couple, and it is the growing expectation of Millennial workers that both partners will work and parent. (HBR article)

- Millennials will make up 75% of the American workforce within 10 years. (HBR article)

- In a survey of 200 human resource managers, two-thirds cited family-supportive policies, including flexible schedules, as the single most important factor in attracting and retaining employees. (White House report)

- In a 2014 study of highly educated professional fathers in the U.S., nine out of ten reported that it would be important when looking for a new job that the employer offered paid parental leave, and six out of ten considered it very or extremely important. These numbers were even higher for Millennial workers. (Department of Labor report)

4 Paid parental leave is important for morale and company culture

- In a study of 253 California firms, only 2–3% of employees were on leave in any given year (for all reasons, not only parental leave).

- 80% of surveyed firms found such policies to be at least cost-neutral, while roughly 50% reported a positive ROI. (White House report)

- Competitive leave policies do not harm productivity or profitability:

"No noticeable effect" or "positive effect" on:	Less than 50 employees	50–99 employees	100+ employees	All employer respondents
Productivity	88.8%	86.6%	71.2%	88.5%
Profitability/Performance	91.1%	91.2%	77.6%	91.0%
Turnover	92.2%	98.6%	96.6%	92.8%
Morale	98.9%	95.6%	91.5%	98.6%

N=175

(sketch space)

DISCUSSION

This presenter did his or her homework. The overwhelming amount of information here could convince me that the parental leave policy needs fixing. But research has shown that piling up evidence doesn't necessarily correlate with increasing persuasion. A few convincing pieces of evidence can be far more effective.

Let's take the slides one by one.

Slide 1: Average comparison. Putting this straightforward data into text form dilutes its power. One of the most common questions audiences will have about data—especially when it pertains to their performance—is *Are we normal?* or *How do we stack up?* So I've quite literally stacked up weeks of leave for this firm against averages. This firm gets color, while averages, because they're not real entities, are gray. The shortcoming comes through much more powerfully here than in the original. Notice that I did not include the last bullet point, about other companies. I thought it would be too much to introduce an entirely new comparison in the same space. This slide is about "our firm" against the average, so I put only that here.

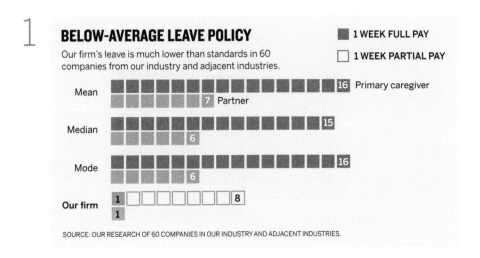

SOURCE: OUR RESEARCH OF 60 COMPANIES IN OUR INDUSTRY AND ADJACENT INDUSTRIES.

One of the most common dataviz mistakes I see in presentations is when presenters try to stuff as many ideas as possible into one chart—or multiple charts on one slide—to keep the slide count down. I'd rather use two slides, each for a single idea or chart, than try to pack in the ideas. And that last bullet point reflects the data that appears in the next slide anyway, so I saved it.

Slide 2: Competitive set comparison. I didn't mind the organization of the original tables, but reading numbers is more laborious than comparing lengths. So I returned to the hybrid bar–unit chart from the previous slide. Units (the blocks representing weeks) help image the numerator; a solid bar turns all those weeks into a single statistic, but units help us think about each week as part of the value. I retained the color scheme so that as the presentation builds, the audience won't have to think about that variable; they'll know what orange and green mean. Typically, I like to create as few alignment points as possible, and here I've limited them, but you'll see that the three qualitative labels ("leading," "good," "lagging") float to the right. I decided that the signal of their relative positions, with leading literally being ahead and lagging farthest back, was more valuable than maintaining alignment for them.

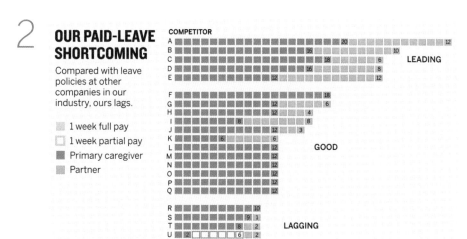

2

OUR PAID-LEAVE SHORTCOMING

Compared with leave policies at other companies in our industry, ours lags.

▢ 1 week full pay
☐ 1 week partial pay
◼ Primary caregiver
▨ Partner

I think this chart could still use some work. On a large screen it would be effective. But I'm concerned about scale and trying to read some of the labels if this is on paper or a personal screen. Even without the labels, though, a clear point comes through: There are three kinds of leave policies, and "our firm" doesn't have the good kind.

You could create suspense by presenting this chart without "our firm's" data and inviting the audience to speculate about which group the firm falls into before revealing the answer. It's a powerful way to keep an audience engaged.

Slide 3: Young talent. I sketched many approaches to this slide and wasn't satisfied with any of them, so I decided to try a simple list with proportional bars. The point, I had said when talking it through with a friend, was to demonstrate a lack of equivocation. Each bar shows that young talent overwhelmingly thinks better leave is a good idea. Taken together, they're a litany of evidence.

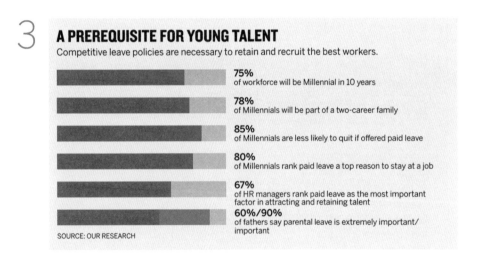

Still, this requires a lot of reading. It comes closest to a traditional presentation slide in its format. The bars are merely suggestions of charts, reminders that the data points to their right—78%, 85%—are big proportions of the whole.

If I were presenting this, I wouldn't take the time to read through each "bullet point." Instead I'd get at the overall idea by saying something like "On all measures, the young talent we're competing for expect a competitive leave policy." (Remember, I've already shown that the firm doesn't offer that.) Then I might choose to expound on one or two data points from the list.

Still, I can imagine that others would come up with different treatments for this data. I look forward to seeing some of them.

Slide 4: Productivity and costs. Because I had established a "litany" approach, I stuck with it. Constantly switching forms forces an audience to repeatedly reset mentally to learn what they're looking at before analyzing it. If they see the same form, they'll know instantly what to do and how to read. In this variation on the theme, I start with a bar chart that shows a very low percentage—a nice way to make people take notice. *This is similar but different—how?* is what their brains will ask when first seeing it.

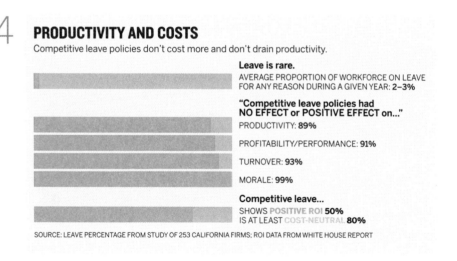

4 **PRODUCTIVITY AND COSTS**
Competitive leave policies don't cost more and don't drain productivity.

Leave is rare.
AVERAGE PROPORTION OF WORKFORCE ON LEAVE FOR ANY REASON DURING A GIVEN YEAR: **2–3%**

"Competitive leave policies had NO EFFECT or POSITIVE EFFECT on..."
PRODUCTIVITY: **89%**
PROFITABILITY/PERFORMANCE: **91%**
TURNOVER: **93%**
MORALE: **99%**

Competitive leave...
SHOWS POSITIVE ROI **50%**
IS AT LEAST COST-NEUTRAL **80%**

SOURCE: LEAVE PERCENTAGE FROM STUDY OF 253 CALIFORNIA FIRMS; ROI DATA FROM WHITE HOUSE REPORT

Overall, I'm building a case by showing data against anticipated concerns: This will cost money. We'll lose productivity. It hurts performance even if it's good for those out on leave.

In anticipation of that pushback, I provide evidence against it. "Actually, it not only doesn't cost money but it shows a positive ROI and is at least neutral on productivity and profitability." Again, in a presentation, it may be powerful to unroll these one at a time by raising the concern and then showing the data that allays it.

Some general points about this entire presentation set:

1. The original presentation, however bloated, was well crafted from a narrative point of view. It flowed smoothly, and that comes through even better when each slide is cleaned up to make its main point more clearly. The flow is something like:

   a. Our firm's leave is below average.
   b. How far below? We are competitive laggards.
   c. That's bad because competitive leave is a crucial talent-recruitment tool.
   d. I know you have concerns about adopting more-competitive leave policies, so let me address some of them.

2. Note that the title and subtitle of every chart serve the same role for that slide as a whole. When you create a blank slide in presentation software, it often prompts you to create a title (and then bullet points), so you do so without thinking. Then you paste in a chart that has its own title, creating clutter and redundancy. There's no need. The chart is the thing!

3. It may be hard to believe, but not much of anything from the original slides has been left out—a valuable reminder that you can present a lot of information clearly so that it doesn't feel like a lot. That makes it more persuasive, because the audience can more readily get to and think about the idea.

CHAPTER 5

CAPTURING CONCEPTS

"The most dubious business plan can look solid—even smart—if it's cast as a virtuous circle."   —Gardiner Morse

THE WRITING PROCESS

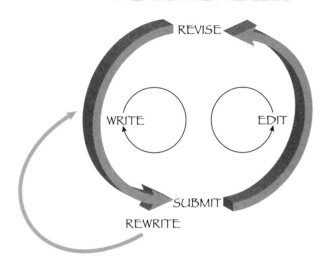

REVISE

WRITE

EDIT

SUBMIT

REWRITE

CONJOINED TRIANGLES OF SUCCESS >>>

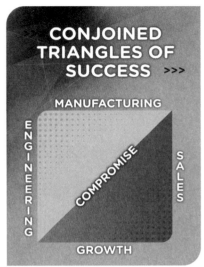

MANUFACTURING

ENGINEERING

COMPROMISE

SALES

GROWTH

COURTESY OF HBO

BUSINESS STRATEGY

REVENUES

PROFITS

COMMUNICATION STRATEGY

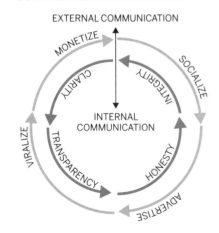

EXTERNAL COMMUNICATION

MONETIZE

SOCIALIZE

CLARITY

INTEGRITY

INTERNAL
COMMUNICATION

VIRALIZE

TRANSPARENCY

HONESTY

ADVERTISE

AT HBR WE CALL THOSE PROCESS DIAGRAMS that show cycles and other neat but meaningless procedures "crap circles," a term coined by senior editor Gardiner Morse. Consultants often peddle crap circles that look lovely and satisfyingly *eternal* but tend to lack usefulness. They may be simple, complicated, or even nested!

You've seen these before, right? It's easy to lampoon such efforts, as HBO did so brilliantly with the Conjoined Triangles of Success on the show *Silicon Valley*, but it's important to understand why they exist—and persist. Crap circles represent one of the more difficult challenges in visualization: non-data viz. Conceptual charts are not bound by statistics, which means they're not bound at all. With no axes or data points, you're free to roam. Find a metaphor you like—a cycle, a target, a spiral, a funnel, a sinking ship—and you can beat that metaphor into the visual. You can add *anything* if you think it will help explain the concept. Anyone who has undertaken a craft—writing, cabinet-making, cooking—knows it's much easier to keep adding stuff in hopes of getting the right things out there than it is to put *only* the right things out there. We are more naturally creators than editors.

But if you can learn to edit yourself, conceptual charts are a powerful tool. At their best, they bring clarity and create memorable representations of abstract ideas. For example, I could try to explain the relationships among the British Isles, Great Britain, the United Kingdom, Ireland, and all other places that have some political affiliation with the United Kingdom, but it's not easy. I could also just show you, on the following page.

BRITAIN AND IRELAND

Understanding the political and geographical
boundaries of the UK and the Republic of Ireland

—— Political boundary
—— Geographical boundary

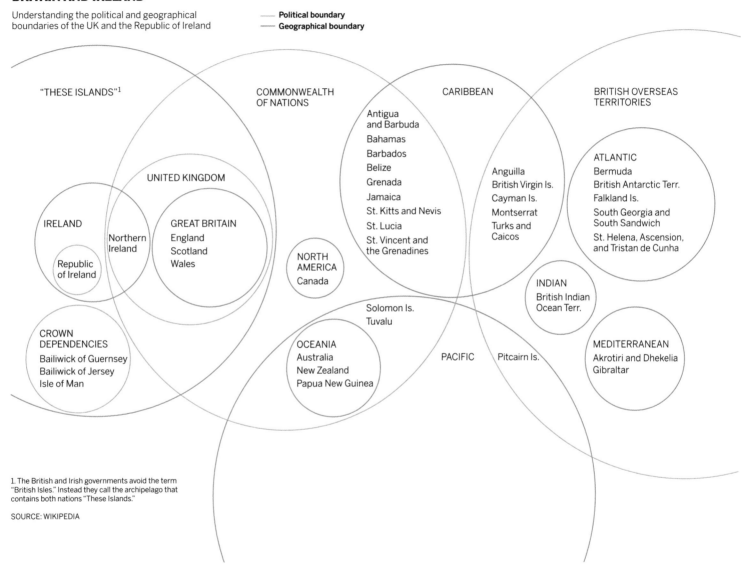

"THESE ISLANDS"[1]

COMMONWEALTH
OF NATIONS

CARIBBEAN

BRITISH OVERSEAS
TERRITORIES

UNITED KINGDOM

IRELAND

Northern
Ireland

Republic
of Ireland

GREAT BRITAIN
England
Scotland
Wales

Antigua
and Barbuda
Bahamas
Barbados
Belize
Grenada
Jamaica
St. Kitts and Nevis
St. Lucia
St. Vincent and
the Grenadines

Anguilla
British Virgin Is.
Cayman Is.
Montserrat
Turks and
Caicos

ATLANTIC
Bermuda
British Antarctic Terr.
Falkland Is.
South Georgia and
South Sandwich
St. Helena, Ascension,
and Tristan de Cunha

NORTH
AMERICA
Canada

CROWN
DEPENDENCIES
Bailiwick of Guernsey
Bailiwick of Jersey
Isle of Man

Solomon Is.
Tuvalu

INDIAN
British Indian
Ocean Terr.

OCEANIA
Australia
New Zealand
Papua New Guinea

PACIFIC

Pitcairn Is.

MEDITERRANEAN
Akrotiri and Dhekelia
Gibraltar

1. The British and Irish governments avoid the term
"British Isles." Instead they call the archipelago that
contains both nations "These Islands."

SOURCE: WIKIPEDIA

You need time to take this in; it's not suitable for a presentation. But in this context, with one set of eyes having the time to connect and learn, it can be clearer and more effective than the text I'd need to explain the various political and geographical relationships.

Follow these guidelines when trying to build conceptual charts:

1 **Avoid mixed metaphors.** A chart meant to show a marketing funnel shouldn't use a cycle diagram. If the title of your conceptual viz is "The Ladder to Success," it shouldn't show stairs. Calling a concept one thing and showing another is a surprisingly common mistake. It's common in writing, too, so surrounding an idea before hitting it directly may just be part of the creative process. I once saw a conceptual visualization titled "Hitting All the Right Notes" that showed a series of events represented by drums—which don't really hit notes. The dataviz maker was thinking about both music and hitting and was getting there. Once you've committed to a visual approach, the key is to make sure the metaphors work.

2 **Restrain yourself.** The urge to decorate conceptual charts is like the urge to use lots of adjectives in creative writing. You may think you're making it artful, but you're actually making it effortful. Color for color's sake, three-dimensionality for objects that don't need it, clip art—you don't need these. Anything that doesn't actively support the idea is distracting. Commit to making your concept clear and stopping right there.

3 **Be less literal.** Just because your marketing plan involves a funnel doesn't mean you need to show an actual funnel. If your idea involves a valley, you don't have to show a river flowing through it or trees along the banks. Absurd? Possibly. But people often explicitly illustrate a metaphor just to make sure the audience gets it. Recently a colleague sent me a conceptual chart showing a funnel with stick-figure customers falling through it. Avoid this. Use shapes and space to just suggest your idea. An upside-down triangle probably suffices for either a funnel or a valley. Parallel lines stacked vertically suggest a ladder well enough.

4 **Stick to conventions.** Just as with statistical charts, heuristics matter. Time generally still moves left to right. Red means hot or danger. Green is good or safe. Hierarchies go from top to bottom. Our minds are so familiar with these ideas that it's disruptive to

change them. Without data to prevent you from twisting things around, though, you may be tempted. Try to use conventions to your advantage rather than undo them.

Here's another convention you can use with conceptual charts: statistical chart forms. Even if you have no data, axes and lines or proportional bars can be effective, because your audience will know that higher on the axis means higher value, or that proportional bars showing a large category and a small category mean "a lot of this and not much of that," even if the relationship isn't statistical. But if you use these, be sure to add a disclaimer to your chart: "Conceptual, not statistical."

5 **Edit yourself.** Editing, another form of restraint, is among the most important and underappreciated skills in chart making, especially with conceptual charts. Deciding to cut back the amount of information you're conveying is hard. We want to impart as much of our knowledge as we can; limiting the number of ideas you present goes against that natural inclination. However, as with writing, editing your charts is both necessary and beneficial. Your audiences won't miss what you don't show them. It's more important to engage them and help them understand, and that's usually easier to accomplish when you communicate a few ideas clearly and efficiently.

6 **Bonus pro tip: Go easy on the arrows.** I've noticed that for whatever reason, arrows tend to be overused and *overdone* in conceptual charts. They're long, or have multiple elbows, or twist like ribbon. Short arrows with fat heads. Long, thin arrows with tiny heads. Arrows with gradient coloring. Even arrows with multiple pointers springing from the center, looking like some mythological chart creature. I'm not sure why people do this. Maybe it's because arrows are sometimes the most eye-catching thing on a diagram otherwise full of text. Your conceptual viz will be cleaner and smarter if you make arrows as short as possible, bend and turn them as little as you can, and keep them in scale.

CAPTURING CONCEPTS WARM-UP

1. Find three elements that make this chart difficult to use and sketch an alternative approach to showing the biological classification system.

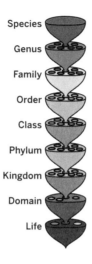

2. You want to show that both sports enthusiasts and hip-hop enthusiasts buy expensive sneakers; both sports enthusiasts and retired professionals invest in high-end televisions; and both retired professionals and hip-hop enthusiasts buy vinyl records. How might you represent these relationships?

3. Sketch a new version of this classic purchase funnel, eliminating all elements you think are extraneous.

4. Maslow's hierarchy of needs is a framework for understanding human motivation. It describes human needs from the largest, most basic ones to more-specific and higher-level ones, which can be met only after the basic needs are achieved. The six levels of his hierarchy, starting with the most basic, are:

1. Physiological
2. Safety
3. Belonging and love
4. Esteem
5. Self-actualization
6. Self-transcendence

Which of the following would be a good conceptual form for showing Maslow's hierarchy?

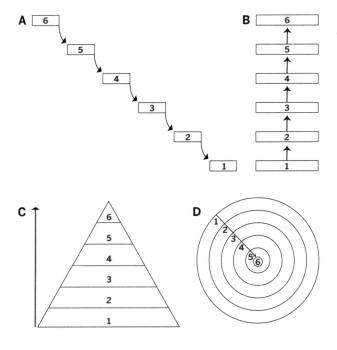

5. You want to design an org chart for your unit. Sketch a basic approach that includes each variable listed here, along with direct and indirect reporting relationships. Group committees and teams however you like.

   2 managers
   5 employees
   2 contractors
   2 liaisons from other departments
   2 committees
   4 project teams

6. The Yerkes-Dodson law suggests that different tasks require different levels of "arousal" to achieve optimal performance. For simple or familiar tasks, we already know that more arousal creates stronger performance. But for complex or unfamiliar ones, performance rises with arousal to a point and then steadily decreases as arousal continues to grow and anxiety takes over. Sketch a representation of the Yerkes-Dodson law that conveys these two ideas.

7. Identify elements that reduce the clarity of this 2x2 matrix and then sketch an improved version.

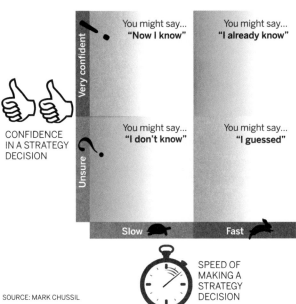

A DECISION-MAKING SPECTRUM

Very confident

You might say...
"Now I know"

You might say...
"I already know"

CONFIDENCE
IN A STRATEGY
DECISION

Unsure

You might say...
"I don't know"

You might say...
"I guessed"

Slow

Fast

SOURCE: MARK CHUSSIL

SPEED OF
MAKING A
STRATEGY
DECISION

8. How might you transform this table into a conceptual visualization?

	BREATHES AIR	CAN SWIM	HAS FINS	HAS LEGS
Chickadee	X			X
Chimpanzee	X			X
Dog	X	X		X
Duck	X	X		X
Earthworm	X			
Jellyfish		X		
Oyster				
Sea anemone				
Sea turtle	X	X		X
Shark		X	X	
Shrimp		X		
Spider	X			X
Stone crab				X
Water moccasin	X	X		
Whale	X	X	X	

9. You want to create a conceptual representation of a product's life cycle showing low sales at introduction, increasing sales through a growth phase, peaking sales at maturity, and declining sales during the last phase. Which representation would you choose?

A **THE PRODUCT LIFE CYCLE**

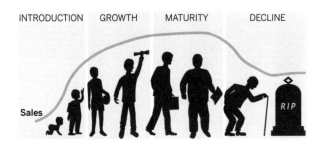

B **THE PRODUCT LIFE CYCLE**

C **THE PRODUCT LIFE CYCLE**

10. Find three elements that make this conceptual chart more difficult to use than it needs to be, and then reinvent it for improved clarity.

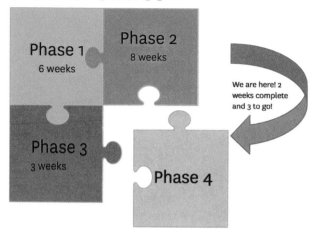

PROJECT STATUS

Phase 1
6 weeks

Phase 2
8 weeks

Phase 3
3 weeks

Phase 4

We are here! 2 weeks complete and 3 to go!

DISCUSSION

1. 1. *Life is at the bottom.* It's unclear what these shapes are, but they look enough like funnels to make the orientation of the strata confusing. Life is the biggest category, comprising all the rest, but those subcategories "funnel down" into life, which is strange. Funnels narrow. Life funnels into animals, which funnel into vertebrates, and so on. Even if we assume these aren't funnels, it's still challenging that all the categories are represented by shapes of the same size and none of them form subsets. We have some good metaphors to work with here: biological classification could be a funnel, or a pyramid, and each category is a subset of the previous, so they are nested. But the visualization doesn't take advantage of any of these ideas.

2. *The rainbow colors.* It's fine to distinguish one category from the next, but it's unclear what purpose these colors serve other than to catch the eye. The rainbow color descends, but why? The similarity of hue in order and class, for example, make me think they're somehow more closely related than, say, order and family. Life and domain appear to be grouped, as do kingdom and phylum and class and order, while the three categories above are more distinct.

Why? I suspect that the chart maker decided to use rainbow colors but had to stretch them because there are more than seven categories.

3. *The dots.* Apparently the dots are meant to show that different levels of classification have different numbers of elements. There are only a couple of kinds of life, so it has fewer dots. But there are many, many families of biological things—so more dots. This chart is conceptual, not statistical, but because I can easily count the dots, I wonder if they are meant to represent some value. I notice them, but I don't readily understand them.

Instead of using color to catch the eye, I've used angled space, which I'd argue is effective enough at getting attention and, unlike the rainbow colors, serves a purpose here. The downward shrinking suggests a filtering to smaller and more-specific domains. Note that the entire visual is enclosed, to give the sense that these entities are not distinct but, rather, subsets of larger entities. Adding an example helps illustrate the concept.

My remake is purposely lo-fi—effectively a table on an angle. I considered other forms: nested circles and an inverted pyramid. But I ran into issues with both: The circles felt complicated and visually busy. The inverted pyramid was close, but descending to the "point" presented labeling problems as the spaces narrowed. So I went with a design that suggests an inverted pyramid but is open enough to accommodate labels.

If you search, you'll find hundreds of designs for biological classification systems and other "pyramid" systems. Many use 3-D perspective to no effect. Often the tiers are colorful to a fault. Trying to come up with something useful but not overdesigned provides a good exercise in restraint.

2. The word overlap sent me right to a Venn diagram. Venns are tricky because they're easy. That makes them overused and misused. Simply overlapping circles doesn't create a relationship between the variables contained in the circles. A commonality must exist to justify the use of a Venn. Also, too much overlap can create patchwork color blending. At that point the dynamic color, rather than the information within the overlaps, becomes the eye-catching element. Here I kept it lo-fi, to suit the very simple message. No color necessary.

BIOLOGICAL CLASSIFICATION WITH EXAMPLE

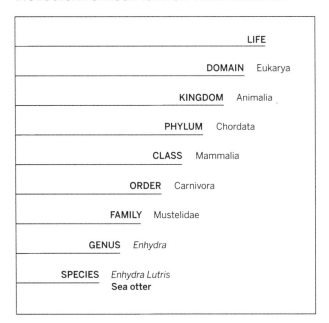

DIFFERENT MARKET SEGMENTS, COMMON INTERESTS

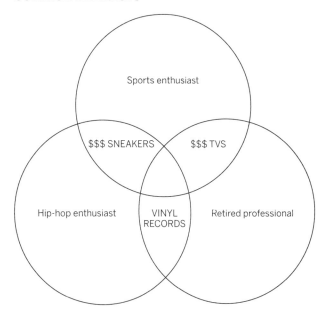

3. Business-process templates like the funnel are easy to find and use. They're eye-catching, but that doesn't always help convey meaning. Extraneous elements in this funnel include the suggestion of three-dimensionality—a more literal interpretation than we need—and its sheen. The bars next to the funnel—presumably for labels—are unnecessary. Words adjacent to the funnel sections would be clearly interpreted as belonging to those sections. Better yet, put the words *on* the funnel—another reason to get rid of the 3-D effect. The colors may be unnecessary as well. Even if you did need color to distinguish, this would force you into five distinct categories. Sometimes a funnel has groups (at the top, at the bottom), which would call for more-complementary colors.

In the spirit of restraint and control, I've reimagined the funnel as simply as possible. I used just six lines to convey the same idea. This still suggests a narrowing; it includes sections; and it will accept labels gracefully. If color is

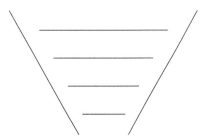

necessary, it can easily be applied to the horizontal section lines. If the title of this were, say, "Our Sales Funnel," there could be no doubt about what it's representing. This is a good example of why it doesn't take much to convey a metaphor clearly. Concepts don't need to be overdesigned.

4. Answer: D. It's another pyramid! Most of the clues were in the wording of the question. "Largest, most basic needs" makes us think of space and foundations. *Basic*, after all, derives from *base*. So we like the idea of that first need being a large base. Then we ascend to "higher" levels. You could also arrive at D by process of elimination. Option A is a waterfall—but the description doesn't suggest that we're falling toward self-transcendence—and it has no scale for the "size" of the need. Option B ascends, rightly, but again, all the needs are equally weighted. Option C is tempting: the base needs are larger, and the concept of aiming at a target for that highest need is appealing. But the descending arrow works against the idea of higher needs. If the labels and arrows started at the bottom and pointed up, this might work. Still, targets aren't quite hierarchies, metaphorically, and given that we have a better option for a hierarchy, I'm sticking with the pyramid.

5. The structure of organizational charts is well established, so I needn't reinvent it. I've stuck to the basic tenets for representing relationships: People at the same level in the organization are on the same plane in the chart. Higher-ups are shown higher up. Solid lines indicate direct reports, and dotted lines indicate indirect reports. For liaisons I chose a curved line to show that the relationship is direct but not part of a reporting structure.

I could have created many more distinct units in this chart. For example, managers' and workers' boxes could have different shapes or weights or sizes. But each additional shape or variable requires viewers to figure out what it represents. Here I use only two types of boxes, for employees and contractors. I've also been careful to keep lines short. Careful observers will notice that I've been consistent with conventions, too. Direct-report lines always enter and exit from the tops and bottoms of boxes, while indirect relationships always enter and exit from the sides. This kind of consistency helps make the chart more readable, even if the person reading it can't say why.

As for teams and committees, I stuck with simple labels rather than try to create visual relationships, which, when I sketched them, quickly became chaotic. I debated color for some time but decided to keep it, because it jumps out a bit more quickly than if everything

was black. I'm counting on the person reading this to get used to seeing Team B as the red team. But by using numbers and letters, I'm also accounting for times when this chart may be printed in black-and-white.

UNIT STRUCTURE

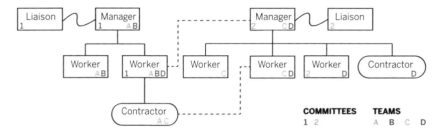

6. Even when you have no data to plot, you can use data-style chart types to convey concepts. Use conventions to your advantage—red means danger, green means safe. Chart types are themselves conventions that you can exploit. Most of us know that a line going up and to the right is usually correlative, and that an outlier in a scatter plot means "this thing isn't like the others." You can use conventions to convey concepts, as I have here. I had no data to chart, but this is how data might look if I could or did chart it. A careful read of the original challenge shows that the language is clearly reflected in the charts.

If you do get in the habit of conveying nonstatistical ideas with statistical chart types, make sure you clearly label them "not statistical," lest someone think there's actual data there.

7. 1. *The title.* We've mixed our metaphors: This is not a spectrum; it's a matrix made from crossing two spectra.

2. *The clip art.* Generally, iconic treatments like this are unnecessary. In this case, they're doubly frustrating, because not only are they redundant decorations but their scale is such that they overpower the labels they're meant to illustrate.

3. *The quadrant labels.* The repeated use of "You might say . . ." doesn't add much here—the quotation marks suffice. Also, why are the labels placed in the top right corners of the quadrants? Does that signify some specific position within the quadrant where those quotations apply, or is it just a design flourish?

THE ORIGINAL YERKES-DODSON CURVE

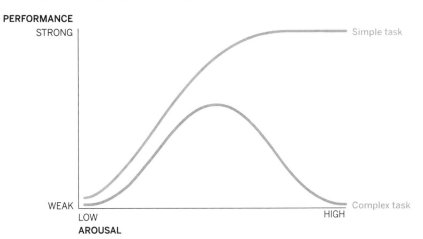

NOTE: CONCEPTUAL, NOT STATISTICAL. SOURCE: ADAPTATION OF A CHART IN THE PUBLIC DOMAIN; WIKIMEDIA COMMONS

4. *The quadrant colors.* Maybe this chart maker wanted to reinforce the idea of a spectrum by using gradient fills for each quadrant. Again, it's unclear whether that serves a function here. The suggestion is that as you move to the right in each quadrant, something changes within that space; but it doesn't. Additionally, the checkerboard color is confusing. Why are opposite ends of the spectrum ("I already know," "I don't know") in the same color family, while the other two contrast with them? This doesn't help us get to understanding. It just raises questions.

To improve on this, I first removed anything that drew the eye but didn't help to tell the story: clip art, extra words, and color gradients. I then used a single color at a different saturation for each quadrant, because there *is* a spectrum embedded in this matrix. It moves linearly from confident/fast, to unsure/slow. Less certainty and speed becomes lighter and lighter. Finally, I changed the headline to better reflect the matrix.

I did very little here beyond editing: most of what makes this better comes from what I took away, not what I changed.

4 STYLES OF STRATEGY DECISION MAKING

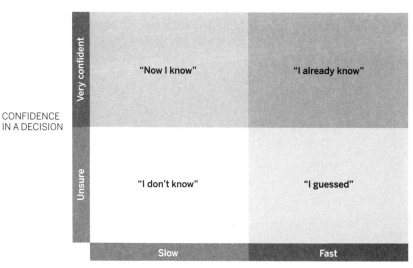

SOURCE: MARK CHUSSIL

8. Matrices of features lend themselves to Venn diagrams. Although some "floating" is inevitable with a Venn diagram, alignment will help. Placing elements arbitrarily creates a sense of disorder. Alignment points in this example make each cluster feel more like a list. A subtle effort has gone into color here: The circles in the blue-green family are things the animals *do*. The circles in the red-orange family are things they *have*.

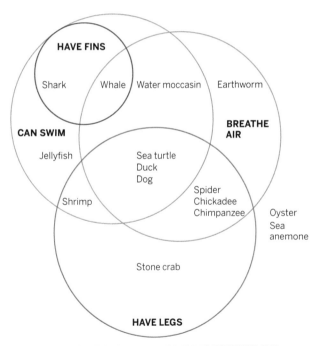

SOURCE: ADAPTED FROM A CHART BY DAVID WALBERT: LEARNNC.ORG/LP/PAGES/2646

Even though the challenge was to visualize the table, a well-designed table may be equally satisfying, depending on context. If you want people to be able to access the individual items first and then see what features they contain, the table is probably a better choice—though it won't be quite as easy to see which items share which features. A diagram will more quickly show features and which items share those features, but finding an individual item and seeing all its attributes won't be as easy—especially as the number of items increases.

9. Answer: C. Despite the phrase *life cycle*, the concept is not truly a cycle. The end does not initiate a new beginning. A life cycle is a progression with a beginning, a middle, and an end. That rules out B, which is a true cycle: the decline phase points at "introduction," which doesn't naturally follow from "decline." Furthermore, the effect of time is relegated to text in the middle. Option A uses the right form but is too clever by half: the phase blocks are OK, but human aging as a metaphor feels disconnected, even inappropriate. Sometimes charts are adorned this way, though, because the alternative (option C) seems too simple. Resist the temptation and trust simplicity.

10. 1. *The color.* It's unclear why the reds get darker with phases, or why phase 4 is an entirely different color. Also, red connotes risk or danger, whereas green connotes safety. In the context of a project status update, this could suggest that the red phases are at risk and that the risk is greatest where the red is deepest.

2. *The arrow.* Its ribbon style draws attention, but it overwhelms the caption, which is the key idea. Also, although it's meant to float without an origin, it appears to be coming from Phase 2, which makes no sense.

3. *The metaphor itself.* Puzzle pieces are a common presentation trope, but they're not right here, because the phases of the project don't interlock and phase 3 isn't connected to phase 2, though it must have followed. Hidden in plain sight is a better concept metaphor: a timeline.

Turning weeks into block units makes the difference between phases clearer. The colors can be reused in later visuals when phases must be recalled in other contexts. The simple equivalence between unfilled blocks and unfinished work is clear enough; I felt it needed no label beyond "We are here."

PROJECT TIMELINE

THE INTERNET OF THINGS LANDSCAPE

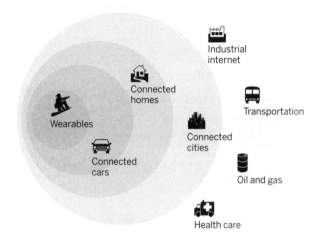

SOURCE: GOLDMAN SACHS GLOBAL INVESTMENT RESEARCH

LANDSCAPES

The big picture. Often we want to show it, but it's difficult. By its nature, it encompasses lots of ideas, long timelines, broad territory. When we try to visualize it, we arrive at the metaphor of a landscape, which makes sense. Landscapes are all the features in a space that's sufficiently grand to suggest what we're trying to show. There's the mobile landscape, the retail landscape, and, as shown here, the Internet of Things landscape. Getting landscapes right requires discipline, editing, and a keen focus on clarity. The easiest approach is to try to create a complete landscape—include everything. But that rarely leads to the best outcome. Let's work on it.

1. Describe what this Internet of Things landscape shows as best you can without any other context.

2. Following is an edited excerpt from an article on HBR.org by Simona Jankowski, a research analyst at Goldman Sachs, which was accompanied by the conceptual visualization shown here.* Given this context, look for ways you might adjust the graphic and sketch a new version based on the text.

> The Internet of Things is emerging as the third wave in the development of the internet. Whereas the fixed internet that grew up in the 1990s connected 1 billion users via PCs, and the mobile internet of the 2000s connected 2 billion users via smartphones (on its way to 6 billion), the IoT is expected to connect 28 billion "things" to the internet by 2020, ranging from wearable devices such as smartwatches to automobiles, appliances, and industrial equipment.
>
> We focus on five key verticals where the IoT will be tested first: Connected Wearable Devices, Connected Cars, Connected Homes, Connected Cities, and the Industrial Internet.
>
> Cars are becoming more connected with each new model, driven by infotainment, navigation, safety, diagnostics, and fleet management. Connected Homes are perhaps the clearest next proving ground for the IoT . . . in areas such as security cameras and kitchen appliances, and the chance to reduce energy use and costs through smart thermostats and HVAC systems.
>
> In connected cities, the U.S. is approaching 50% penetration of 150 million total endpoints. In Europe there is a target for 80% of households to have smart meters by 2020. Smart meters and the grid network architecture lay the foundation for further connectivity . . . including smart street lighting, parking meters, traffic lights, electric vehicle charging, and others.
>
> We believe the Industrial IoT opportunity could amount to $2 trillion by 2020, impacting three main areas within industrials: building automation, manufacturing, and resources. Factories and industrial facilities will use the IoT to improve energy efficiency, remote monitoring and control of physical assets, and productivity.

3. Find another simple conceptual chart in the article text and sketch a version of it.

*Simona Jankowski, "The Sectors Where the Internet of Things Really Matters," HBR.org, October 22, 2014.

(sketch space)

DISCUSSION

The easiest thing to do with a landscape diagram is to treat it like a realist's landscape painting and include everything: foreground, middle ground, background. Tiny details. This usually leads to cluttered and confusing charts. A common example is the "brand landscape" that dumps dozens of company logos into a space to show all the players in an industry arranged with some organizing principle—low-end versus high-end, for example.

I applaud this Internet of Things landscape for avoiding the fate of many landscape charts, but I wonder whether it hasn't swung too far the other way, becoming so simple that it's unclear again.

1. With no other information available, I suspect that we're looking at size of markets for various Internet of Things categories. That would explain the growing circles moving outward. The largest circle represents the entirety of the IoT landscape, and the smaller ones show subsets of the market. That doesn't explain the progressive saturation of blue, which I suspect is meant simply to distinguish the space within which each subset lives.

    This may seem like an unfair prompt—to interpret a chart without all the information—but it's actually a useful one. Show friends a conceptual chart absent any context and ask them what they see. You shouldn't expect them to readily get it, but the process will expose weaknesses. They may keep seeing something you didn't intend, or they may miss the one thing you wanted them to get right away. That's what happened to me with this graphic.

2. The text accompanying the graphic reveals a time element I didn't pick up on. Not only is the overall market growing but there are existing markets and potential markets, generally moving outward—though not exactly. Some areas are partly developed; some haven't yet arrived. I would think about a more explicit treatment of time here and then see if I could find a way to represent the overlapping nature

of what's real and what's to come in the verticals. The year 2020 seems like a good anchor to use as my "future point," since it's mentioned twice.

I found it interesting that the article calls them "five key verticals" but represents those verticals with *circles*. I would try some other ways to show the segments.

The text mentions specific endpoints and potential market sizes, but I might shy away from getting too specific in my conceptual diagram. I would probably try versions with and without the data points, but my initial inclination is to stick with generalities, because the numbers are future focused and neither comprehensive nor consistent. Not every vertical includes an estimate, and some are in endpoints while others are in dollars. The text can get into the weeds.

What you're reading here is the kind of constructive crit you can and should apply to your charts and others. It sounds almost like sketching in my head, and that's what it is. I react quickly to what I see without overthinking it. I capture some of what I say, circling keywords in the text, sketching alternative approaches. It's a habit worth developing. Just as good writers are great readers, good chart makers are great chart users. Practice helps.

In the end, I didn't change much here, because the concentric circles were a strong starting point. But I think it improves clarity just enough to mark an improvement. By adding the axis labels, I've made clear what the dimensions of the shapes represent. The demarcation helps put overall development of the IoT landscape in context. The overlap of the growth is intentional, showing how the sectors tend to interact and connect with one another. And finally, by using horizontal space, I've created room in the landscape to add information—about the applications within each vertical, for example.

THE INTERNET OF THINGS LANDSCAPE

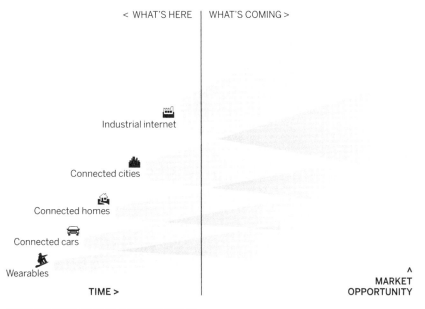

SOURCE: GOLDMAN SACHS GLOBAL INVESTMENT RESEARCH

Improvement doesn't always come from adding more details to a conceptual chart. Sometimes just a few of the right details will transform it from too restrained and vague to crisp and clear.

3. I saw multiple opportunities for conceptual charts in the article text. I seriously considered a Venn with circles for the five verticals that would enclose applications and benefits. But I couldn't pass up visualizing the first paragraph. The wave metaphor jumped out at me, and all the elements for visualization are right there. There is some data, so in a sense this is a hybrid conceptual-statistical chart. I consider it more conceptual, because we don't actually know what the growth curves look like— we only know the proportional difference at the endpoint. I made no effort to create true curves and instead approximated what smooth growth would look like. I did not label the y-axis, because the true numbers are less important here than the idea of each wave's growth rate. Crucially, I noted at the bottom that this is conceptual. The end result is a simple chart where you can see three waves, with one ready to wash over us, and I reinforced that idea in the title.

THE INTERNET'S THIRD WAVE IS A TSUNAMI

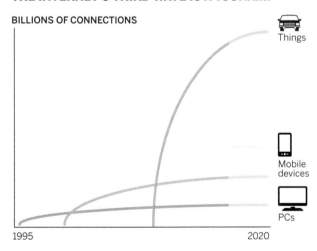

BILLIONS OF CONNECTIONS

Things

Mobile devices

PCs

1995   2020

NOTE: PROPORTIONALLY ACCURATE CONCEPTUAL REPRESENTATION
SOURCE: GOLDMAN SACHS GLOBAL INVESTMENT RESEARCH

TIERS AND TIMELINES

Let's tackle two of the most common tropes in business presentations: tiers and time-lines. Services come in tiers; organizations have tiers; there are tiers of influence and tiered pricing models. Strategies unfold over time; programs and products roll out over time; the history of a company is a timeline. Hell, a revenue chart is a timeline, ripe for marking up with key events that influenced the trend line. At some point you'll be called on to explain some tiered model and to make a timeline. It will help to have effective strategies for these common forms.

The two-slide presentation here shows both tiers and a timeline as part of a pitch to a company thinking about investing in a sales training program. The slides are comprehensive, but are they effective? Both allude to tiers, and the second slouches toward visualization, but I think we can improve them. Let's work on it.

1. Visualize the ideas in the first slide. Use as much or as little information from the slide as you think necessary.
2. Critique the timeline in the second slide. Find elements you think are effective, elements you think are ineffective or confusing, one thing you'd add or change, and any other ideas you think are worth capturing.
3. Reimagine this presentation using conceptual visualizations. Use as many or as few slides as you think necessary to be effective.

Proposed Sales Training Program
Reaching multiple tiers in the organization

Executive Sales Leadership Series (October–December 2017)

For Executive Leadership (about 10 people)
- High-touch personalized event for the most senior members of the organization, with fine accommodations
- 5-day in-person retreat and 2-day end-of-series in-person gathering
- Includes lectures, small-group work, strategy development, network building, and coaching

Sales Management Program (January–June 2018)

For Elite Sales Team (about 25 people)
- Immersive learning session for Hi-Po sales staffers
- Designed to help build the executive leadership pipeline
- 3-day in-person seminar and 1-day end-of-program gathering with virtual learning in between

Sales Staff Capabilities Development (February 2018–January 2019)

For Sales Staff (about 100 people)
- Virtual learning module for larger group and self-directed study and learning
- Includes live lectures, on-demand access, study materials, and video lessons
- 4-week virtual program

Proposed Delivery Road Map   Proposed timeline

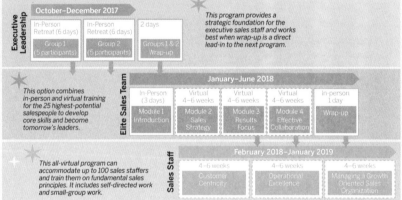

(sketch space)

DISCUSSION

Sales is a high-stakes game. The intense pressure to convey information that will make a sale can lead to information overload. Although including everything ensures that you'll include the right things, it's counterproductive, because it leads to overburdened slides like these. To present these is to invite the audience to read and not listen. But as impossible as the situation may seem, you're starting from a good point: you have strong metaphors to build concept charts on, and the information, despite appearances, is well organized.

1. If you study the original first slide, you'll find there's plenty of structural thinking going on. The tiers are there, as bullet-point units, and the indentation suggests different levels within the organization—almost as if the chart maker was thinking about an org chart. The sales staff reports up to the elite sales team, which reports up to the executive team.

    But the text betrays this hierarchy, because the number of people grows as you descend the tiers. Equal space is devoted to unequal cohorts. The biggest group is put in the smallest width.

My approach was to focus on one simple visual of tiers: the classic pyramid. It was hard to escape this idea once I saw that the number of people grows as we descend the tiers. This is a classic case for a pyramid structure. I also considered three unit charts—one with 10 dots, one with 25, and one with 100, stacked up. In the end I decided that wouldn't convey hierarchy quite as well as the pyramid, and—as you'll see—it wasn't as reusable in this context.

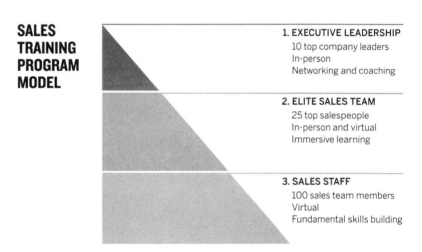

SALES TRAINING PROGRAM MODEL

1. EXECUTIVE LEADERSHIP
10 top company leaders
In-person
Networking and coaching

2. ELITE SALES TEAM
25 top salespeople
In-person and virtual
Immersive learning

3. SALES STAFF
100 sales team members
Virtual
Fundamental skills building

I halved my pyramid vertically—that creates a nice left alignment point and doesn't waste space. Numbering the wedge titles cues the audience that the progression is top down, not bottom up. My biggest challenge was what to do with the bullet points spatially. At first I aligned them snugly along their wedges, but that created multiple alignment points and an emphasis on the diagonal that was visually distracting. Aligning the text creates the problem of pushing the top wedge far away from its text, so clean stroke lines maintain the connection without overpowering the visual.

Finally, I wanted to see how few words I could retain without losing what I felt was the crucial information in the original slide. I'm always aggressive in these exercises, and I've been accused more than once of going too far and losing necessary words. I'm comfortable with what's left here if this is a presentation slide. Notably, this slide manages to communicate most of what the original did, but the original used 138 words. This uses 35. Remembering that I can fill in some details as I talk—and the audience will listen to me because they won't be busy reading the slide—I opted for retaining just three bits of information in each tier: who, how, and what. I omitted the time frames. I was thinking ahead to the timeline, knowing that information was over there, too. However, if this chart needed to stand alone, restoring the time frames would be advisable. I expect that many who try this challenge will retain the timeline, which is not a bad choice.

The overarching idea here is to be bold with the visual, because the metaphor is so simple and strong, and minimize all other distractions.

2. What I found effective:

- *I like the use of colors for each tier in the timeline.* It makes sense to keep them consistent and makes it easy for me to know where to look. And they're reusable— anytime I'm talking about one of the three groups, I can use its color to create a quick, subconscious association.
- *I like the use of different box styles for in-person and virtual sessions.* Using a dashed outline for virtual sessions made sense without much thinking. I just got it.

What I found ineffective or confusing:

- *The starred paragraphs distracted me from taking in the timeline.* I felt the conflict between reading the text and understanding the visual. What's more, once I had read them, I felt cheated. The text either repeated information from the previous slide or described in text what the timeline shows.
- *The downward arrows confused me.* I wasn't sure whether they were meant to map to the timeline literally or just to show a general progression from one tier to the next. The gray doesn't read well against the colors, either. I almost overlooked the arrows.

What I want to add or change:

- I want the timeline to be more *timeliney*. Good information is packed in here, but the relationship between the progression of time and the events within isn't clear to me. For example, the bottom tier, for sales staff, covers 11 months on the timeline but includes only three modules of 4–6 weeks across that space. Using space proportionally for real time and program time would make this more effective.

Other ideas worth capturing:

- I often use this category to collect my nitpicking—small details in design and execution. Here I noted two. The sideways text feels like a design flourish not worth keeping. And the boxes themselves may be overengineered, with a scheme that requires colored text in the white fields and white text in the colored fields. I'd look to simplify that.

A crit like this is invaluable for developing good visualization habits. It helps you think about what you're looking at and also find your voice. The more you do it, the more you'll notice that you tend to like or dislike certain approaches and that your adjustments consistently map to a certain style or technique you find effective.

But remember, a critique is not a grade. Mine isn't *right*—it's just my honest first reaction to what I'm looking at. You may think the starred paragraphs are effective. That's fine. Use critiques as an opportunity to think and learn rather than to judge. You'll notice that I didn't refer to things as wrong or bad above. I talked about what worked for me and what didn't, and what I felt when looking at the visualization. The best crits are in this vein.

3. I turned the two original slides into 10 slides. Yes, 10. You may blanch at that number, but I hope that when you see how I've constructed them, it will make sense. I'll break up the discussion by slide sets.

Tiers. I created a four-slide run to show the tiers. Slide 1 introduces the tier concept and includes no further detail. Each successive slide focuses on one tier, and the information presented is consistent with that for other tiers.

This is subtly different from the classic "building slide." Instead of piling new information on top of old, I do something subtly different. At each step new information is introduced and old information is removed. This forces focus. Only what I want to talk about is there for the audience to think about. That creates opportunities for focused discussion. If all three tiers were visible and I were talking about tier 1, nothing would stop an audience member from reading ahead, raising her hand, and asking about tier 3.

When executed well, this will feel like one slide that changes three times rather than like four separate slides. It's among the most powerful techniques available for presenting dataviz.

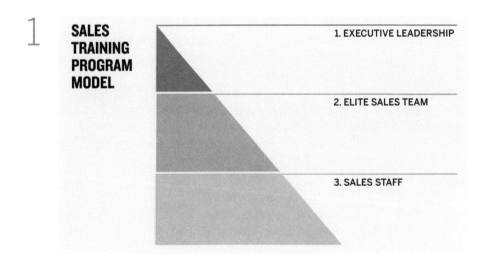

2

SALES TRAINING PROGRAM MODEL

1. EXECUTIVE LEADERSHIP

10 top company leaders
In-person
Networking and coaching

3

SALES TRAINING PROGRAM MODEL

2. ELITE SALES TEAM

25 top salespeople
In-person and virtual
Immersive learning

4 SALES TRAINING PROGRAM MODEL

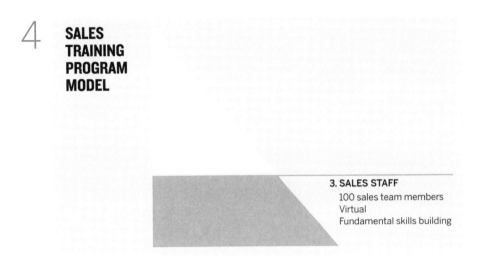

3. SALES STAFF
100 sales team members
Virtual
Fundamental skills building

Timelines. I reused the forced-focus technique for the timeline but employed a couple of added ideas. First I needed to distinguish between in-person events and virtual events. In the original, boxes were outlined with either a solid or a dotted line. I took inspiration from that and used crosshatching to show virtual events versus in-person events. Labeling each type once is enough to lock it into the audience's memory. (Notice that I didn't use a key but, rather, labeled real instances, to limit eye travel.)

Next I wanted to rationalize real time, so I created a true timeline by making event time proportional within real time. The benefits of this exceeded my expectations. It clearly shows the allotted time span and provides a nearly instantaneous sense of each tier's relative intensity. Tier 2 appears to be a very deep commitment, relatively speaking. Also, since I'm pitching a client, I don't have real dates for these events, so the white space becomes negotiable. Maybe the client wants tier 3 to start later; it's now obvious that's possible. Maybe the client thinks tier 2 is too intense and wants to extend that timeline.

I matched colors with tiers to make explicit the connection between who and when. I also brought the tiers back as landmarks to remind viewers of the connection.

Again, if executed well, this will feel not like four slides but like one slide that changes three times.

5 SALES TRAINING PROPOSED TIMELINE

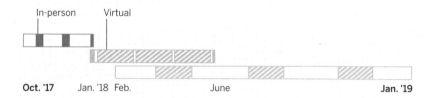

In-person   Virtual

Oct. '17   Jan. '18 Feb.   June   Jan. '19

6 EXECUTIVE LEADERSHIP TIMELINE

Two 6-day in-person retreats (5 execs per)
One 3-day in-person capstone event
Capstone coincides with launch of tier 2

Oct. '17   Jan. '18 Feb.   June   Jan. '19

7 ELITE SALES TEAM TIMELINE

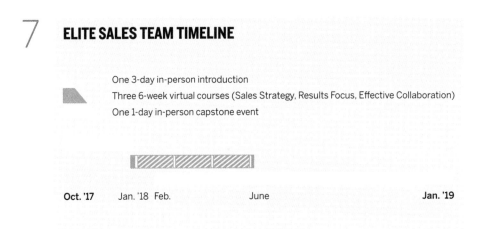

One 3-day in-person introduction

Three 6-week virtual courses (Sales Strategy, Results Focus, Effective Collaboration)

One 1-day in-person capstone event

Oct. '17   Jan. '18 Feb.   June   Jan. '19

8 SALES STAFF TEAM TIMELINE

Three 6-week virtual courses (Customer Centricity, Operational Excellence, Growth Orientation)

Oct. '17   Jan. '18 Feb.   June   Jan. '19

Leave-behinds. Two of the 10 slides I made were not for the presentation but for the paper version of it that I will leave behind. In a live presentation I have seconds to get people's attention and help them understand. I can't afford to present dense slides with many charts that require explanation. But if the viewers are reading on their own, on a screen or on paper, the sparse presentation slides may not be enough of a guide for them. They can control the pace, so I'm afforded the luxury of layering more detail into one space.

To that end, the "two-second" versions of the material in the presentation become "two-minute" versions on paper or a personal screen. For the tiers, the slide is identical to the presentation series but merged in one space. For the timeline, I reused my original version showing the entire timeline and added details underneath, again reusing the tiers as landmarks.

A final note on "leave-behind" slides. When you're presenting, don't hand them out in advance. If you do, the audience will ignore you and flip through the materials in front of them, formulating questions based on their personal interpretation. You may even be answering their questions in your presentation, but they're not paying attention. We all do this. Just hold off and promise you'll provide them with detailed slides when the presentation is over.

SALES TRAINING PROGRAM MODEL

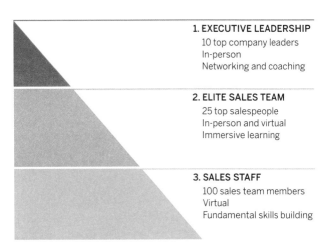

1. EXECUTIVE LEADERSHIP
10 top company leaders
In-person
Networking and coaching

2. ELITE SALES TEAM
25 top salespeople
In-person and virtual
Immersive learning

3. SALES STAFF
100 sales team members
Virtual
Fundamental skills building

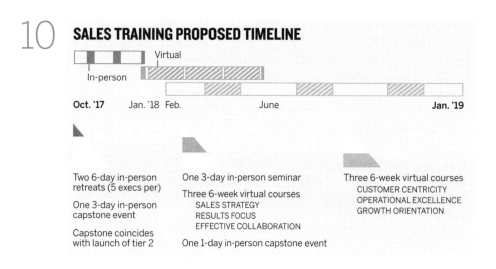

SALES TRAINING PROPOSED TIMELINE

Virtual

In-person

Oct. '17   Jan. '18   Feb.   June   Jan. '19

Two 6-day in-person retreats (5 execs per)

One 3-day in-person capstone event

Capstone coincides with launch of tier 2

One 3-day in-person seminar

Three 6-week virtual courses
SALES STRATEGY
RESULTS FOCUS
EFFECTIVE COLLABORATION

One 1-day in-person capstone event

Three 6-week virtual courses
CUSTOMER CENTRICITY
OPERATIONAL EXCELLENCE
GROWTH ORIENTATION

Even now, that number, 10 slides, probably makes some readers uneasy. It's just not how we make presentations. But I urge you to try this approach. You may be surprised by how effective it is. When I give data visualization presentations, I use these techniques. Afterward I often ask the audience how many slides they think I presented in a 30-minute talk. Answers range from 20 to at most 70. On average, my presentations include more than 120 slides. My principle is simple: I'd rather use 10 slides that each take 10 seconds to present than two slides that require five minutes to unpack. When you shift the unit of measure from a slide to an idea, and when you use multiple slides to build an idea, people stop thinking about how many pages you're going through, because they're utterly engaged.

OUR SCRUM PROTOCOL

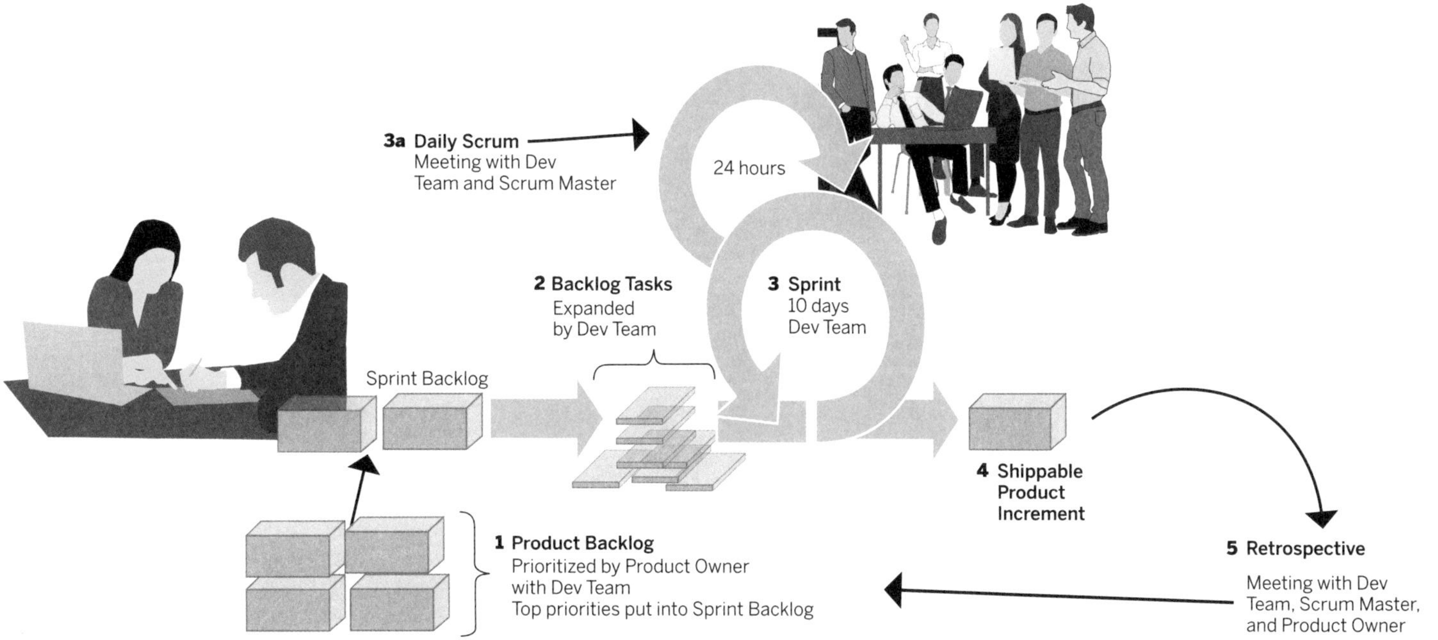

3a Daily Scrum
Meeting with Dev
Team and Scrum Master

24 hours

2 Backlog Tasks
Expanded
by Dev Team

3 Sprint
10 days
Dev Team

Sprint Backlog

4 Shippable
Product
Increment

1 Product Backlog
Prioritized by Product Owner
with Dev Team
Top priorities put into Sprint Backlog

5 Retrospective
Meeting with Dev
Team, Scrum Master,
and Product Owner

SOURCE: ADAPTATION OF A CHART BY MAREKVENTUR (OWN WORK), VIA WIKIMEDIA COMMONS

PROCESSES

Just how does an agile development scrum process work? Executives must want to know, because the internet is full of charts devoted to trying to explain it. Most follow a structure similar to what you see here, though I've mashed several of the takes I found into one big muddle. It bears some of the hallmarks of a typical conceptual visualization for a presentation, such as clip art and plenty of fancy arrows. But as a process diagram, it suffers from a lack of clarity. Multiple metaphors (cycles, blocks) combine to create a difficult experience. Let's work on it.

1. What is the best primary metaphor to use for this scrum process—a timeline, a cycle, or a step-by-step? Why?
2. Find one element to eliminate and two elements to adjust to make this visualization clearer.
3. Sketch a new version of this scrum process that improves its clarity, given the following added information:

   • The sprint backlog is made up of high-priority products.
   • A product is made up of tasks (which are features and fixes) that are "sized" differently depending on the work required to complete them.
   • Incomplete tasks are what's developed during sprints.
   • Shippable product increments are completed tasks, integrated into the product.

(sketch space)

DISCUSSION

I believe this is the most difficult challenge in the whole workbook. Even in this simplified view of scrum, so much is happening, involving different teams and time frames, that it's hard to keep it all straight. In some conceptual diagrams the metaphors are off or the design is counterproductive, but the core of a good idea is buried in the mess. Here multiple issues have to be unpacked, and no obvious solution is hiding in plain sight.

1. I chose a cycle. The diagram contains all three metaphors. The step-by-step is the numbered process. The timeline is both explicit in the looping sprint and implicit in the overall left-to-right development process. The cycle, though, overrides both, because the steps form the cycle, and a timeline is part of that cycle. The green looping arrows look like cycles, but they're not the cycle we're focused on (we're not even sure from this diagram why those arrows loop); the black arrows form the cycle. It was difficult to see this because that cycle isn't the most visually prominent element. It's not even shaped like a cycle. It's good practice to explicitly state what your main metaphor is and then make sure it's visually dominant in your conceptual viz.

2. 1. *Remove the clip art.* This one was easy. I appreciate what the chart maker was trying to do: the clip art suggests the activity at the step it's placed near. And because we don't yet understand the process, we try to use this clip art to inform our developing sense of what we're looking at, but it doesn't help much. It makes a complex diagram needlessly busier. A subtle point: the clip art is pasted in at different scales. That creates a depth of field, so the group of people in the back look farther back. It can suggest there's depth to the process diagram as well. If illustrations are added to a flat diagram, it's best to make them the same scale.

    2. *Adjust the title.* Once again, the metaphors have been mixed. We're looking at a process, not a protocol. More specifically, we're looking at a development cycle. It would be better to go generic here ("How Do We Scrum?") than to use the wrong nomenclature.

3. *Adjust the arrows.* Some process diagrams require many arrows, and those arrows may have to bend or twist or travel long distances. That's okay. We just want them to be as efficient as possible. Here there are two issues to address. First, the loops have to be rationalized. What do they mean? Are they necessary? And why are they different from the other arrows? I think there's a reason for it: my guess is that the green arrows reflect development, while the black ones represent planning and meeting. Still, I'd like to think about how to make that distinction without having one set of arrows be so dominant. Second, I should clean up the black arrows. They're haphazard. None is level. The curved one is an outlier.

3. I don't think I got this right. My visualization falls short in key areas that I'll discuss. I look forward to seeing your solutions, submitted to GoodChartsBook@gmail.com, and I suspect many of them will improve on this significantly. I kept it as is to show a work in progress and to demonstrate that visual challenges often have no easy solution. Sometimes you have to compromise, or sacrifice, or rethink your goal of visualizing a complex system that resists a clear visual treatment.

I managed to reconcile all the processes embedded in the original, and the key was to focus on the two separate activities occurring: planning and development. I then reduced the overall cycle to its simplest form as a three-step process: plan and prioritize; sprint; review.

OUR SCRUM DEVELOPMENT CYCLE

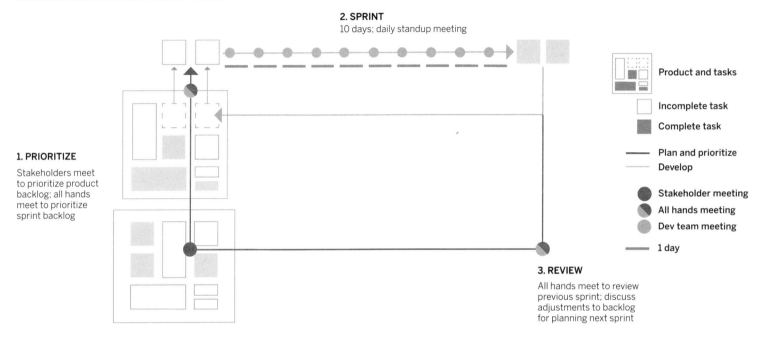

2. SPRINT
10 days; daily standup meeting

1. PRIORITIZE
Stakeholders meet
to prioritize product
backlog; all hands
meet to prioritize
sprint backlog

3. REVIEW
All hands meet to review
previous sprint; discuss
adjustments to backlog
for planning next sprint

Product and tasks

Incomplete task

Complete task

Plan and prioritize
Develop

Stakeholder meeting
All hands meeting
Dev team meeting

1 day

Then, instead of trying to create the whole visual, I took on the three parts of the
process separately. I started with the sprint, which itself was a cycle within the
cycle. Incomplete tasks go in; they're developed over 10 days, with meetings to
discuss progress every day; and completed tasks come out. Those completed tasks
are integrated back into the product, and new incomplete tasks are queued up for
development. I struggled here primarily with representing the timeline and the
daily stand-up. My days were mostly blocks that looked too much like the tasks. My
sketches are full of tunnels and other ideas, but I settled on a simple dotted line,
which I felt suggested a conveyor belt carrying the task to completion. You'll notice

that the double loop is gone completely. I was never happy with it, nor was I certain what it means. The backward-looping 10-day development arrow with a counter-vailing 24-hour loop (nearly the same size, which was strange) is just odd. My sense is that the sprint loop is meant to represent the cycle of finishing a sprint, going back to take on new work, and repeating. You can see the confusion in the original diagram—it's unclear how to follow the various paths. When do I get off the loop and finish a task?

Next I took on the prioritize section. In the original diagram I was confused by the similarity of all the blue blocks except for the "slices" in the sprint backlog. To under-stand what was really happening, I had to do research, reflected in the additional information I provided. With this information I was able to come up with a reason-ably simple approach to representing products and tasks. I decided to make this part vertical to reflect high-priority items going into the sprint. Still, I'm not satisfied with the process overlay, or with the clarity of the finished tasks going back into the product. Is it clear enough that the process determines when those two tasks are put into the sprint? Putting them back appears to be going backward in time, against the sprint. Once again, representing the sprint time frustrated me.

Finally, I took on review, the simplest because it's just a meeting that reignites the process. It was when I thought about the review point that I decided meeting points could be just that—points on the cycle.

I see plenty of cues that I don't have this right yet. The size and complexity of the key suggest that I'm working with too many variables (and it creates lots of eye travel). The amount of text at each point in the cycle suggests that the visual isn't quite doing its job. And the tension between the timeline in the sprint and the direction of the process arrows still seems confusing.

It could be that this process is too complex for one diagram. I felt more comfortable when I was designing just the sprint visualization, or the backlog visualization. The struggle came when I had to put them together. If I wanted to keep going here, I might try to make a series of diagrams rather than just one.

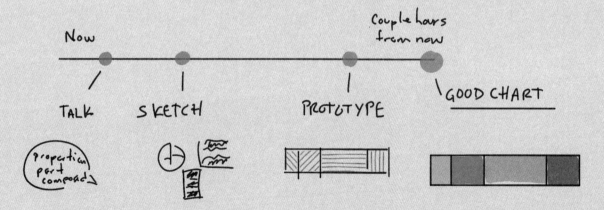

PART TWO

MAKE GOOD CHARTS

Now .... Couple hours from now

TALK   SKETCH   PROTOTYPE   GOOD CHART

proportion part compoad

CHAPTER 6

TALK, SKETCH, PROTOTYPE

"Sometimes you want to give up the guitar, you'll hate the guitar. But if you stick with it, you're gonna be rewarded." —Jimi Hendrix

WHEN YOU LEARN TO PLAY THE GUITAR, you have to learn scales, chords, chord changes, strumming patterns, and fingerpicking. You build these skills (and others) so that when they're combined, you can play songs and, eventually, use what you know to make your own music.

If you've gone through the Build Skills section of this book, you've put in quite a bit of practice. Now you'll play some songs and, finally, make your own music. The songs will be already-completed chart challenges that you can practice on. The music will be your own data and ideas put through the process that will make them good charts.

In these challenges, you'll use the techniques we've captured so far—color, clarity, chart types, persuasion, and concepts. You can put them all together now. The goal in these challenges is to arrive at good ideas and sketches or paper prototypes of good charts. Make sure your context is well set—that you know what you're trying to say, to whom, and in what setting you'll be saying it. Then design your chart to convey that context effectively. This is the framework laid out in the original *Good Charts*.

Step I: Talk

Put aside your data and find a friend. Have a conversation to set your context. Start by stating what you want to show. Other questions to address: *Who is this for? What do you want them to do after seeing this? How will it be displayed? If you could show them only one thing, what would it be? Do they already understand this, or is it new to them? Will it be surprising or affirming? Do you need to persuade them?*

Any question that helps you define what you need to show will be useful. Make sure your friend asks *Why?* constantly. Forcing you to state even the obvious will surface hidden assumptions. If you say, "I need them to understand the trend," your friend might say, "Why?" and you may think the answer is so obvious that the question is dumb. Answer it anyway. You may find yourself saying, "If they understand the trend, we can finally wake them up to the potential risks"—which is a great contextual clue about what you're *really* trying to accomplish.

During this process, capture words and phrases that are visual, such as *huge gap* or *the trend line shows a big dip*. Also capture phrases that might describe the approach you want to take. For example, if you say, "I need them to understand that sales change seasonally, in a predictable cycle starting with a summer dip," you've given yourself lots of information about where to start, what variables to use, and what you need to show overall.

Usually this step lasts about 15 minutes. You'll know you're ready to move on if the conversation ebbs or you feel that you're repeating yourself.

Step 2: Sketch

As you're talking, start to sketch possible approaches. Go fast. Don't worry about being messy. Don't worry about real values or labels. See how different chart types and layouts might work with what you're doing. Scribble a bar chart and think about what the x- and y-axes would be. Doesn't work? How about a scatter plot? What would the dots represent, and could you color code them? Try at least two different approaches, just to keep your mind open. Can you tell a story? Write down "setup," "conflict," "resolution," and sketch what you might show at each step. Or just capture keywords for each step of the story. Example: *Setup:* "Show revenues." *Conflict:* "Mark on line where hacks happened." *Resolution:* "Show revenues after hacks."

The key is to keep moving. You want to be generative, creating ideas rapidly. Continue talking through the process, and as new ideas and visual words come up, jot them down. In a short time you'll have an idea of where you want to go. You'll know you're ready to move on when you find yourself focusing on trying to improve one sketch or one idea instead of coming up with new ideas. This step overlaps with the talking step and usually lasts anywhere from 10 to 30 minutes for a couple of charts, depending on the complexity of what you've taken on.

Step 3: Prototype

Whereas sketching is fast and open, prototyping is a bit slower and more deliberate. The first prototype can be a paper one: a neat sketch. Now you should use neater axis lines and try to approximate plotting real values. Use color purposefully. Sketching is generative; prototyping is iterative. Hone your chart until it approaches good. If your data is in a spreadsheet format such as XLS or CSV, you can plug it into any number of visualizing tools to make digital prototypes. I often use Plot.ly as a starting point for prototyping. If you're conversant with more-advanced tools like Tableau, or statistical packages like R, you can use those as well. The key is to test color schemes, labels, and other elements to make sure they'll work in a final design and that you're seeing what you thought you'd see when they're rendered. I've found that depending on how well I hit the mark talking and sketching, time for prototyping can vary widely. When you've hit the mark, it might last 20 minutes. But when prototyping unveils flaws in your thinking, you may go back to talking and sketching and then return to prototyping for another 40 minutes or longer. You want to exit prototyping confident in your approach, ready to make a final chart.

Use this process as dictated by the challenges following. I'll provide the conversations that provide context. You may have to choose between the best outcome for color and the best for persuasion. Or you may believe you have the right chart type but it lacks clarity. One of the great insights when you tackle any craft is that you rarely achieve perfection. You make trade-offs. You sacrifice here to benefit there. Or you decide that the cost of investing in something, while it might be nice, isn't worth it. This is utterly typical, and okay.

CHAPTER 7

THE MONTHLY REPORT

Subscription Production Update

Our goal was to go from 7,000 to 10,000 subscriptions during this year-long period of subscription production.

Annual and two-year subscriptions made up most of the new subscribers during the year, and monthly and lifetime options even had some zero-add or negative months when they lost subscriptions.

Most of the growth came from annual and two-year subscriptions, although other subscription types also had net positive results during the year.

SUBSCRIPTIONS (THOUSANDS)

	Aug. 2016	Sept. 2016	Oct. 2016	Nov. 2016	Dec. 2016	Jan. 2017	Feb. 2017	Mar. 2017	April 2017	May. 2017	June 2017	July 2017
Total	6.55	6.85	7.15	7.60	8.55	8.50	9.00	9.55	9.90	10.20	10.70	11.15

■ Annual   ■ Two-year   ■ Monthly   □ Lifetime

TOTAL NEW SUBSCRIPTIONS	300	300	450	950	–50	500	550	350	300	500	450	4600
Annual	100	100	200	250	250	250	350	200	200	350	250	2500
Two-year	50	100	100	100	100	100	150	100	50	100	50	1000
Monthly	50	50	50	50	50	50	50	50	—	50	50	500
Lifetime	100	50	100	550	–450	100	—	—	50	—	100	600

THE MONTHLY REPORT

Here it is: the classic data dump. The bosses want an update on The Numbers, so that's what the marketing manager at a podcast app company creates: a single slide showing all of them. The manager needs to update her supervisor about subscription production every month, and this is the slide she uses. The company offers four subscription options and has target goals for growth. In addition to totals by month, her boss likes to see how many of each type of subscription are added each month. Recently he complained about the chart, saying it was confusing, and annoying to deal with. Even reading it by himself on his screen, the boss said, was frustrating. The marketing manager wants to remake her chart to impress him next month.

To improve it, we're going to talk, sketch, and prototype. The talking has already been done, by me and my friend the marketing manager. Review this conversation. Mark it up with notes; highlight visual language and cues that will help you create an alternative. Sketch your solutions until you feel you have an improved approach, and then create a paper prototype of your version of the monthly report.

"So, what are you working on?"
"I need to improve this chart, because my boss finds it confusing and frustrating."

"How?"
"He says he has a hard time reading it and can see other people in the room tuning it out because they just read the captions and then wait for the next slide."

"Why is this chart important?"
"Are you kidding? This is *the* monthly update. This is how they know how we're doing with subscriptions."

"How are you doing?"
"Good. We've surpassed our target of 10,000 subscriptions. We were slightly below target a year ago; now we're slightly above."

"Why, do you think?"
"That's the best part—we've improved mostly in the two subscription categories we want to grow: annual and two-year. I mean, they're all important, but we really want to focus on those two as the most important, sort of versus the other two, because annual and two-year are our most profitable subscriptions."

"What are the others?"
"Monthly and lifetime. Monthly is hard because it requires renewal each month, so there's more turnover. And lifetime is nice because once you have those customers, you have them. But they can cancel, and it's definitely not our most profitable option."

"Was there a promotion or something that caused the growth to exceed your goal?"
"No, it's been steady growth, which is great. We did one promotion on lifetime subscriptions, and it looked like it worked—they jumped up. But then a bunch of people canceled almost immediately because they just didn't see the value, so that category actually dropped the very next month."

"That seems important to show."
"Not really. They know about that disaster of a campaign. We learned a lot, but I'd rather focus on the steady growth in the categories we want to grow."

"So why not just show that? Get rid of everything else?"
"I can't do that! They need the other information, too."

"What other information?"
"They need to see the portfolio of subscriptions and how they're trending. All at once, in one place, stacked up against each other."

"Why?"
"Why? This is the monthly update. They want to see an *update*, not just the good news I want to show them. I can highlight the steady growth, but they want all the data."

"Do they want to see each subscription type more than the total? Which is more important?"
"Both are important. They want to see everything."

"But if you had to choose, which would you choose?"
"I can't choose! They need to know it all. Total. How we're doing against our goals. How each type is doing. And my boss is really interested in seeing a breakdown of monthly subscription adds."

"Why?"
"Well, it's one thing to just show a total, but people cancel, too. So net adds are important. If 100 people cancel and 150 subscribe, that's a plus-50 net add. He likes to see that. That's why I put the big table there. It has every data point, so he knows if any subscription category has negative net adds, which would raise a red flag."

"So that's the most important thing?"
"For him, maybe, but he's not the only person in the room. It's all important. Why do you keep forcing me to say what's most important?"

"I look at your chart and think it's just trying to do so many things. I don't know what's most important. By making it all important, you keep me from seeing any one thing that I'm supposed to focus on. I don't even see the goal at all."
"Well, the goal isn't really in the spreadsheet, so we never think to make it part of the chart. I just put it in the caption. But we should probably show the goal. I know what you mean about it doing all this different stuff; but like I said, I need to show more than one thing. I suppose I could take each part of the data one by one. I just haven't figured out how."

"Do they need to know every month's specific value, as you've labeled?"
"I think they like having that."

"Why?"
"It just seems like something that's good for them to have. I mean, they really care about the trend more than anything. That's how they think—in trends."

"Maybe it's making it confusing here, and you could give them the table afterward and just focus on the trend line?"
"Yeah, maybe. Never thought of that."

"OK. The only other thing I don't get is the table. It's so much information for a presentation. I just wonder if there's a visual way to do that."
"I was thinking about that. I tried to line it up so that each month is underneath the label for the month in the bar chart, to make that connection."

"I didn't get that at all. But now I see it."
"Oh. That's not good. I think what he does is try to eyeball how many adds we have each month in annual and two-year subscriptions and how many adds we have in the others and compare those. He wants to make sure there's healthy production in annual and two-year. And you can see in the second half of this report, that really started to happen."

"I don't actually see it without your telling me that."
"OK. So I need to show that better, too."

"Yeah, I think it's all here, but let's just start sketching some ideas on how to show everything while showing one thing at a time so that it's not all jumbled together. I'm imagining trying to look at this on a screen and get the idea during the presentation. I'd have a hard time seeing some of the trends you point out. The one that jumps out at me is the overall steady growth, but it's hard to see where that's coming from within the categories with all those little labeled slices."

"Yeah, let's sketch and try some things."

(sketch space)

DISCUSSION

Instead of marking up the conversation in this scenario, I'm going to present my notes from each part of the process as they unfolded. The first set of notes represents what I wrote down during the conversation. Remember that talking and sketching usually overlap, even though I present them sequentially. Also note that some of the sketching time was used to mark up the original chart with ideas and comments. I often do that as a form of visual critique and to connect ideas in the conversation to the existing chart. I look for places where the conversation seems to be supported by what's shown and places where I don't see what we're talking about. As you proceed through the discussion, note:

1. *The process of capturing keywords, phrases, and ideas from the conversation.* Sometimes I underline for emphasis, or note how many times a phrase comes up, telling me it's important. You'll also see quick sketches near some of the keywords, and lots of question marks, which I use to indicate where I still have questions or to prompt myself to explore further.

2. *How messy my sketching is.* I'm purposefully incautious—I'm just seeking a general direction. Although I use some color, I try to limit it to the essential so that I'm not spending sketching time choosing colors. I just want to make distinctions that I can focus on later, during prototyping. Sometimes I repeat keywords near my sketch to remind myself of the connection between what we talked about and what we're trying show. I also put stars next to things I like and something else next to ideas I don't like to indicate that I've ruled them out.

3. *The relative neatness of the prototype.* It's by no means perfect, but I'm being more careful and thinking more deeply about color, labels, and arrangement on the page.

4. *The changes between prototype and final product.* The first prototype guides the final product, but I'm still making adjustments to layout and color decisions as I see them unfold in the final chart.

Talk

The notes show just how much of this conversation was visual. Words and phrases popped: *steady growth*, *stacked up*, *passed the target*, and, most notably, *trend line*, which came up in various forms four or five times. This was especially instructive because no trend line was to be found in the original chart. I noticed that performance against goal seemed to be important, but the target goal wasn't a visual element; as my friend had acknowledged, it was buried in a caption. I was intrigued by the table, because she could explain to me exactly how she thought her boss was using it, and that led to several ideas about ways to make this crucial information more usable and more visual. Her explanation that it was meant to connect to the bar chart by

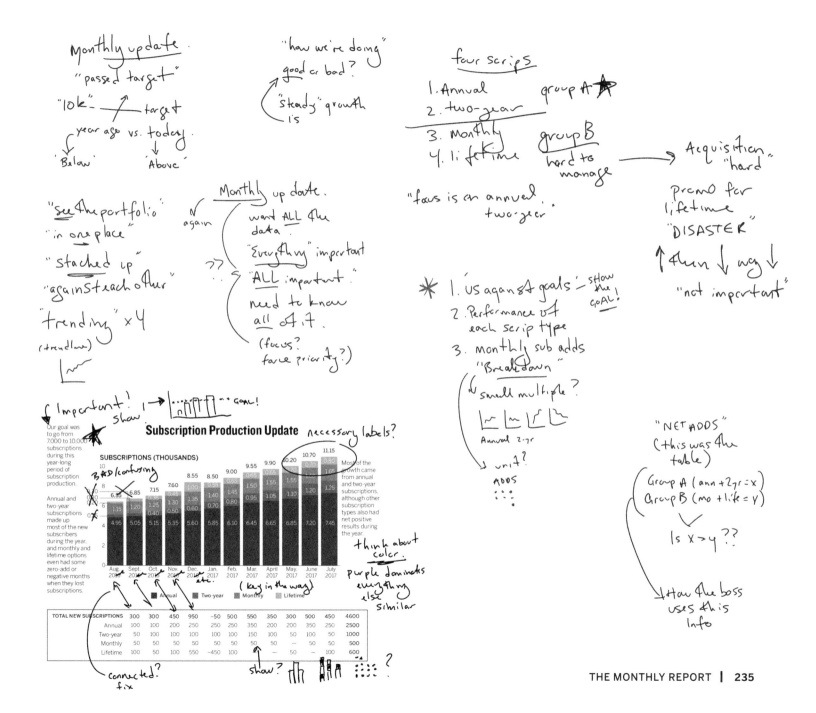

x-axis dates was a surprise, because the bar chart's key completely broke that connection for me. And since the table was so important, I felt it could be improved on; I was already thinking about how to visualize it. I also started marking up some obvious design shortcomings in the original, such as the x-axis labels and the bar section labels.

My friend got frustrated by my repeatedly asking what was most important—and I got frustrated by her continually telling me that *everything* was important. This is typical in such conversations. The inclination is to leave everything in, both to show our work and because we truly believe that everything is important. Challenge yourself to prioritize information and have the courage to simplify. Showing all the information isn't an advantage if it makes the chart impossible to use.

We finally broke the stalemate when we jointly identified the *three* ideas that the *one* chart and *one* table were meant to convey. We realized that everything could be equally important—we just didn't have to put it all in one space. So we set about thinking through the three ideas marked by the red star in my notes.

Sketch

Sketching attacked the three ideas in order. First, we wanted to see the trend line against goals. So we literally sketched those two things and looked at

the result: simple, and it explicitly shows a *comparison between* where things stood and the company's goals. I was confident this was the way to go, but we also jotted down a couple of other ideas. My friend suggested adding a goals trend line to the existing bars because it was *easy*. I don't mind that in a time pinch, but I thought it might draw attention to the pieces of a bar rather than to the total bar against goals. I also wanted to see if showing the distance between results and goal each month would work. That would create a lollipop chart with several floating bars. The distance between the performance point and goal point each month would be instructive concerning how far off targets the company was each month. I think this would be an effective approach in some contexts, but here it shifts the focus to making comparisons in individual months rather than seeing the *trend*—that word that came up so often. So we nixed it; starred the first, simple approach; and moved on.

Our second idea was to show each subscription type against the others. The original does that, but the notion of those two groups we talked about (annual and two-year versus monthly and lifetime) doesn't come through, largely because of color. In the original I see "purple" and "the others." So we spent time thinking about how we might color code the bars to make them more effective. But I was eager to get away from bars. Bars are good at encouraging comparisons. They invite us to compare October with November, March with April, and so forth. The trend! We kept coming back to the trend. If we used a line chart for the first idea, why not

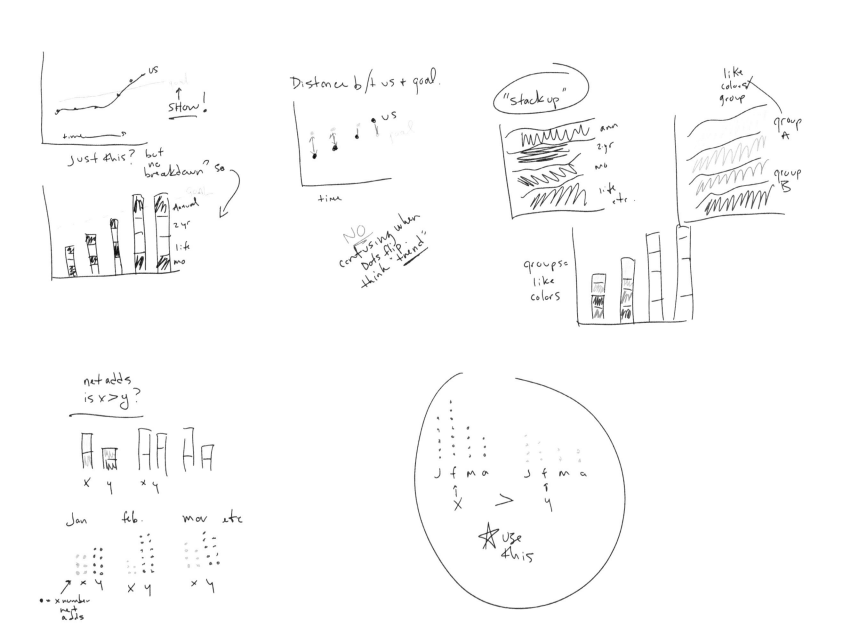

another? It would almost feel like a *breakdown* of the overall trend in the first chart—and *breakdown* was precisely the word we used in our conversation. The phrase *stacked up* also kept coming back, so I scribbled a stacked area chart just to think through how that might work. If we got the color right, it might. That was the key. We wanted to compare two groups of two, not four different subscription options. So we scribbled in a blue/orange color scheme, and even as we sketched it, we felt confident it would work. So we moved on.

The third idea, showing net adds, didn't come easily at first. We thought we might reuse the stacked bars, since individual months were more important than the trend line in this data. Remember that her boss liked to see each month's performance and wanted to compare the performance of the two groups. At first we just stared for a few minutes. In my notes I rendered her boss's intent as a simple equation question: Is x > y? We knew we needed to show x and y and be able to compare them. We had no other ideas for side-by-side comparisons of the two groups. During a lull we returned to the conversation notes. Nothing popped, and we felt stuck. Often, if the numbers I'm dealing with aren't large or complex, I like to at least try a unit chart. Unit charts assign values to individual marks to make the numbers seem more concrete. Here a dot could equal some number of new subscriptions. So I started stabbing at the page, making dots—first one color and then another as a comparison. What if every dot equaled, say, 100 subscriptions? We

agreed that this was worth pursuing and quickly sketched a couple more, liking that the dots looked like bar charts but also had that sense of units. Then I tried combining the two groups next to each other, x in one set and y in the other. Is x > y? There it was. We were ready to prototype.

Prototype

The paper prototype here (yes it's a digital file, but it's a neat sketch and was created by hand, like a paper prototype) went quickly. We neatened up the axes and approximated real values. Colors were purposeful and consistent throughout—two groups of opposing colors so that viewers could still see all four variables but look at them as two groups. On the unit chart, given all the repetition of the original x-axis, I decided to use a label common in charts—just the first letter of the month. If these unit charts sit with the other charts, I decided, that would work; but I made a mental note that if they were separated, longer abbreviations might be better. The prototype confirmed that we had hit on something that increased clarity but didn't sacrifice much information in the original chart. This prototype was followed by a few digital prototypes (not pictured here to save space and because they incorporate only small tweaks) that were converted to SVG files and polished up as our final product: a new monthly update for the boss that would be easier to understand and more usable.

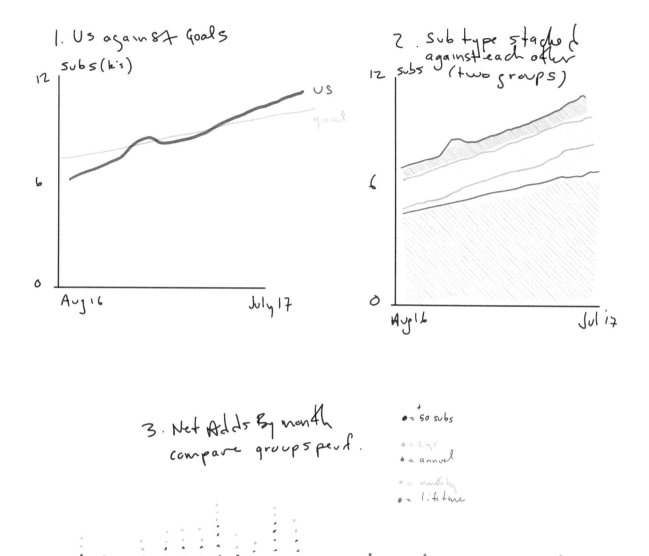

1. Us against Goals

subs (k's)

12

6

0

Aug 16   July 17

US

goal

2. Sub type stacked against each other (two groups)

12 subs

6

0

Aug 16   Jul 17

3. Net Adds by month
compare groups perf.

• = 50 subs

• = 2 yr
• = annual

• = monthly
• = lifetime

A S O N D J F M A M J J   A S O N D J F M A M J J

SUBSCRIPTION PRODUCTION: AUGUST 2016–JULY 2017

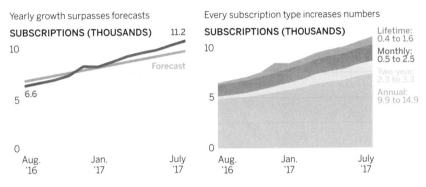

Yearly growth surpasses forecasts

SUBSCRIPTIONS (THOUSANDS)   11.2

10

Forecast

5   6.6

0

Aug.   Jan.   July
'16   '17   '17

Every subscription type increases numbers

SUBSCRIPTIONS (THOUSANDS)

Lifetime:
0.4 to 1.6

Monthly:
0.5 to 2.5

Two-year:
2.3 to 3.3

Annual:
9.9 to 14.9

10

5

0

Aug.   Jan.   July
'16   '17   '17

Annual, two-year options make up 75% of net adds

SUBSCRIPTIONS (THOUSANDS)

O +50 new subscribers

A   S   O   N   D   J   F   M   A   M   J   J
'16   '17

Two-year:
NET ADDS 1,000

Lifetime
NET ADDS 600

Annual
NET ADDS 2,500

Monthly
NET ADDS 500

Good Charts

Those three ideas are so clearly executed here that it's hard to imagine people getting confused or tuning out of the monthly update. I can picture each of these as its own slide in a presentation setting. The consistent use of color trains the audience on what greens mean and what oranges mean, no matter where they go in the presentation. We switched from blue to green, and looking back, we're not sure it was the best choice. The oranges seem to dominate the greens. We talked about it, but we didn't have the time then to go back and tweak. We might do so now. Notice, too, that the unit chart changed: we switched to comparing each month's x and y rather than a full year's x and a full year's y from the prototype. When we got close to the end, my friend said that her boss likes to make these comparisons monthly—indeed, she had said that in the conversation. So we made the switch. In fact, we tried it three ways. Here are the other two, for comparison.

I could make an argument for any of the three depending on context, but I'm happy to stick with the month-by-month comparison we ultimately chose to use.

Having the whole process laid out here should help you see the progression of ideas, and why that conversation is so crucial. Throughout the process those keywords and ideas kept coming back to inform the chart types we tried, the ways we organized the information, and even the tweaks we made to the final product. The conversation was the well we kept going back to draw from; whether we were stuck or flying forward, it's what impelled us. Start with a few words and a few scribbles; you'll find you're already much closer to a good chart than you think.

SUBSCRIPTIONS (THOUSANDS)

● +50 new subscribers

A S O N D J F M A M J J
'16   '17

TWO YEAR
NET ADDS

ANNUAL
NET ADDS 2,500

A S O N D J F M A M J J
'16   '17

LIFETIME
NET ADDS 600

MONTHLY
NET ADDS 500

SUBSCRIPTIONS (THOUSANDS)

● +50 new subscribers

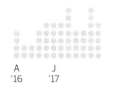

A   J   A   J
'16   '17   '16   '17

ANNUAL
NET ADDS 5.4k

TWO YEAR
NET ADDS

A   J   A   J
'16   '17   '16   '17

MONTHLY
NET ADDS 1.2k

LIFETIME
NET ADDS 1.1k

CHAPTER 8

THE PLASTIC PROBLEM PRESENTATION

THE PLASTIC PROBLEM PRESENTATION

This challenge combines something from nearly every skill covered in this book, notably choosing chart types, crafting for clarity, and practicing persuasion. Science and research teem with data, and this particular data set, from an important paper by Jennifer Lavers and Alexander Bond, published by the *Proceedings of the National Academy of Sciences of the United States of America* (PNAS), contains some of the most eye-popping data about plastic garbage you'll ever find.*

In reporting the data for a journal, the job of the authors is not to persuade us of anything other than the veracity of their findings. Your challenge is how to honor their science while making a case to a lay audience. How far can you push the "pop treatment" of academic research? What are some visual approaches that will get people to *feel* the scope of the problem and the volume of plastic we're talking about here?

Scenario: You need to give a presentation that will persuade an audience of nonscientists that the problem of plastic waste in the South Pacific is critical. Using the data collected in this research, put together a series of visualizations to tell the story of the Plastic Problem. Use the talk-sketch-prototype method. Study the data and then talk to a friend about how you might show some of the findings. Capture the visual words and ideas you find yourself saying aloud. Sketch possible approaches to visualizing the data. Think about how you'd arrange your visualizations in a presentation for maximum impact with a lay audience.

*Jennifer L. Lavers and Alexander L. Bond, "Exceptional and Rapid Accumulation of Anthropogenic Debris on One of the World's Most Remote and Pristine Islands," *Proceedings of the National Academy of Sciences of the United States of America*, May 15, 2017. The data I present here is a simplified version of the report's data. For the purposes of making the challenge manageable, I've rounded values and left out margins of error. I've also omitted some other categorizations of the debris including its size and location. For those who are interested in this topic, I recommend reading the full paper and the extensive coverage of it in the media.

Henderson Island 2015 Plastic Waste

		NORTH BEACH	EAST BEACH	
Density (Items / m²)	Surface	30	239	
	Buried (to 10 cm)	209	2,573	
Number (Total pieces)	Surface	800,000	3,100,000	
	Buried (to 10 cm)	6,900,000	27,000,000	
	TOTAL	**7,700,000**	**30,100,000**	**37,800,000**
Mass (Kg)	Surface	3,000	12,600	
	Buried (to 10 cm)	97	1,100	
	TOTAL	**3,097**	**13,700**	**16,797**

Plastic Waste Sampled, 1991 vs. 2015

	DUCIE & OENO ATOLLS 1991 (AVERAGE)	HENDERSON ISLAND 2015
Disposable		
Caps & lids	75	486
Plastic bottles	66	115
Plastic bags/Pieces		60
Pen lid	3	10
Drinking straw		10
Plastic razor		4
Cigarette lighter	4	3
Toothbrush		2
Plastic cutlery		2
TOTAL	**148**	**692**
Fishing Related		
Cord & rope	48	3,336
Strapping	8	642
Crates/Pieces	7	245
Fishing line		220
Netting		207
Buoy	123	50
Buckets/Pieces	3	25
Glow sticks		16
TOTAL	**189**	**4,741**
Other		
Fragment	287	48,121
Resin pellets		6,774
Fencing		121
Melted plastic		43
Pipe	28	27
Tiling spacer		3
TOTAL	**315**	**55,089**
TOTAL FRAGMENTS SAMPLED	**652**	**60,522**

(sketch space)

DISCUSSION

I love this challenge. It's wide open. It lends itself to any number of interpretations and chart types. The numbers are dramatic, offering plenty of opportunities to use compelling storytelling techniques. The way I solved it will most likely differ radically from the way you do. Implicit in this challenge is an important data visualization lesson: most of the time there isn't one right answer, one right chart. And most good answers involve trade-offs. Usually we're picking between good options, each with its strengths and weaknesses. For example, as you'll see in my solution to this challenge, I sacrificed precision in my representation of the data for an overall feel. This helps make a compelling narrative, but I lose access to clear representations of actual values. You could easily go the other way and sacrifice the story for a comprehensive, orderly arrangement of all the values represented in the tables. Neither approach is "correct." Acknowledge that the approach you take will always have pluses, minuses, and trade-offs. Don't focus on finding the *right* chart. Focus on finding a *good* chart.

Here's how I attacked this challenge.

Talk

I spoke with a friend for about 15 minutes after having studied the data for about 20 minutes. She immediately noticed some of the negative words I was using, such as *horrible*, *unimaginable*, *gross*, and *awful*. She pressed me on that, asking why it was so, so bad, although the answer seemed obvious to me. But it was a good question. It forced me to explain, out loud, what I was thinking: that all this trash had accumulated in the past 25 years—it hadn't always been there. It drew me to the idea of a before-and-after narrative.

Much of the rest of our conversation focused on how the trash was distributed. Words like *strewn* and *covering* and *accumulation* were captured as ways to describe what I needed to show. My friend asked if it mattered to me that some of the plastic was buried and some was not. I said yes. She asked why. I didn't have a good answer for her, but I was convinced that I wanted to show both. She asked if the different types of plastic mattered. "I guess," I said. I was sort of interested in breaking down the types of plastic the researchers had found, but I also felt some indifference. I just knew that I wanted to focus on the raw number of pieces of plastic found on the island in some way, then and now.

Another theme that kept coming up was the difference between North Beach and East Beach. East Beach was much worse. "Does it matter why it's worse?" my friend asked. "No," I said, "but I think it's interesting to show both separately. It could add to the drama to show North Beach first, which is bad, and then East Beach, which is just unfathomable."

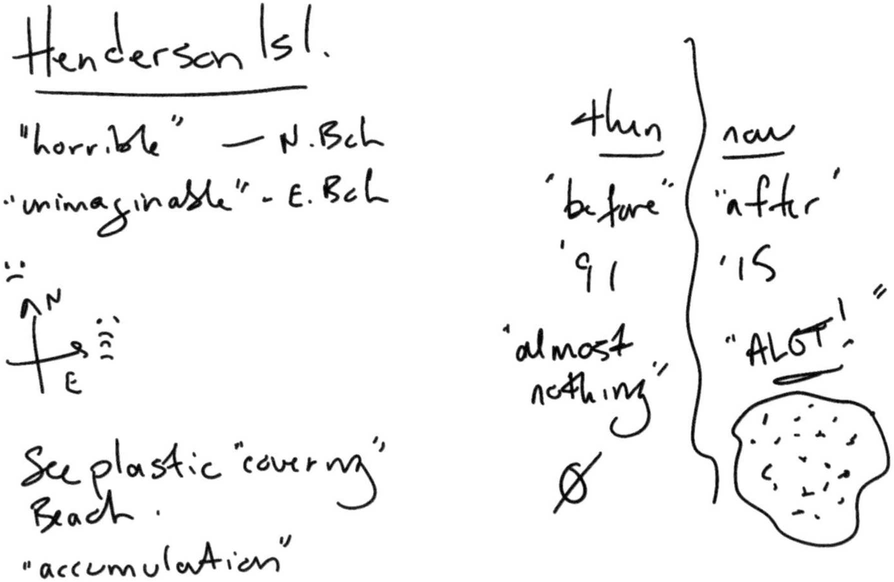

Henderson Isl.
_____

"horrible" — N.Bch
"unimaginable" - E.Bch

See plastic "covering" Beach.
"accumulation"

then | now
"before" | "after"
'91 | '15
'almost nothing" | "ALOT!"
∅

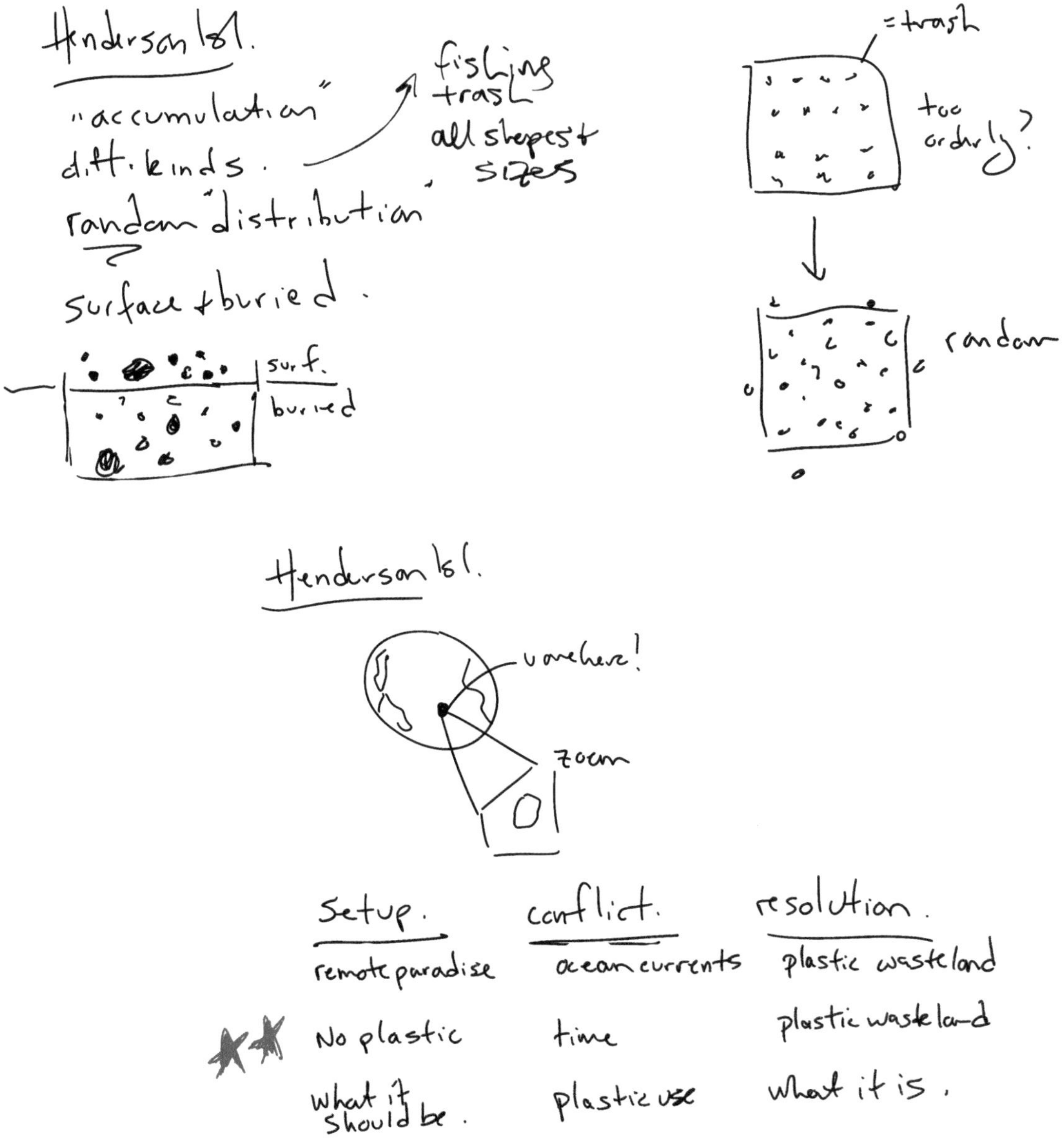

Henderson Isl.

"accumulation"
diff. kinds.
random "distribution"

fishing
trash
all shapes +
sizes

surface + buried.

surf.
buried

= trash

too
orderly?

random

Henderson Isl.

u are here!

zoom

Setup.	conflict.	resolution.
remote paradise	ocean currents	plastic wasteland
No plastic	time	plastic wasteland
what if should be.	plastic use	what it is.

Sketch

Even while chatting I was thinking about using a stretch of beach for my primary visual approach, orienting the water in my picture by its orientation in the real world. My early efforts focused on simply re-reporting the data visually. Most of the results are reported in items per one meter squared, so that's where I started. I also immediately tried to combine as many variables as I could in this one space. I figured I could put dots on the beach to represent plastic items and then use color and size to represent other variables, such as the type of plastic.

At this point I had no idea what the real data would look like in the space, and I was insisting to myself that placing the dots randomly would be better than an orderly distribution. I wasn't even sure how I'd accomplish that. Still, I kept going. I force myself during sketching to refrain from refining too much. I'm trying to get lots of ideas out there. To test my instinct, I quickly sketched a more orderly set of dots as a bar chart to show the breakdown of types of plastic, but I didn't think it would work, because the difference in values between the totals for 1991 and those for 2015 was so big that some would have just a few dots and some would have thousands.

The difference in numbers also led me to consider scaling up my visual space. I wanted to create a strip of sand that showed more of the beach. One square meter is fine, but I thought people would relate better to a bigger space, and of course that meant plotting more pieces of plastic. I toyed with nine square meters, or maybe even 81. I also decided that at this point, to help people relate to the space, I'd need some point of reference for size. A person, for example.

I liked this, but I realized that I was creating work for myself. The data was reported in values of one meter squared. Now I'd be multiplying that data. To get to a good chart, I often find myself adjusting the base unit of the data or otherwise manipulating what's at hand. I have to consider how much time I have, of course, but often I find it's worth it to bring the data into a more accessible form.

At this point I also started thinking about buried plastic, and I remember shaking my head over how I would show items in three-dimensional depth. I have some design skills, but I wasn't sure I could do that. I decided to put it off until I started prototyping. If I couldn't pull it off in a prototype, I'd come back to sketching.

For breaking down the plastic waste by type, I really wanted a treemap. A square would echo the square of beach space I wanted to show in the distribution plots and would allow for hierarchy in the data: one box could represent "fishing" plastic, and within that I could put "netting," "cord," and so forth. I sketched a variation on this using circles within circles, and as a hedge, I unpacked those circles in another attempt—a much simpler treatment—in case the treemap didn't work. In every case I was

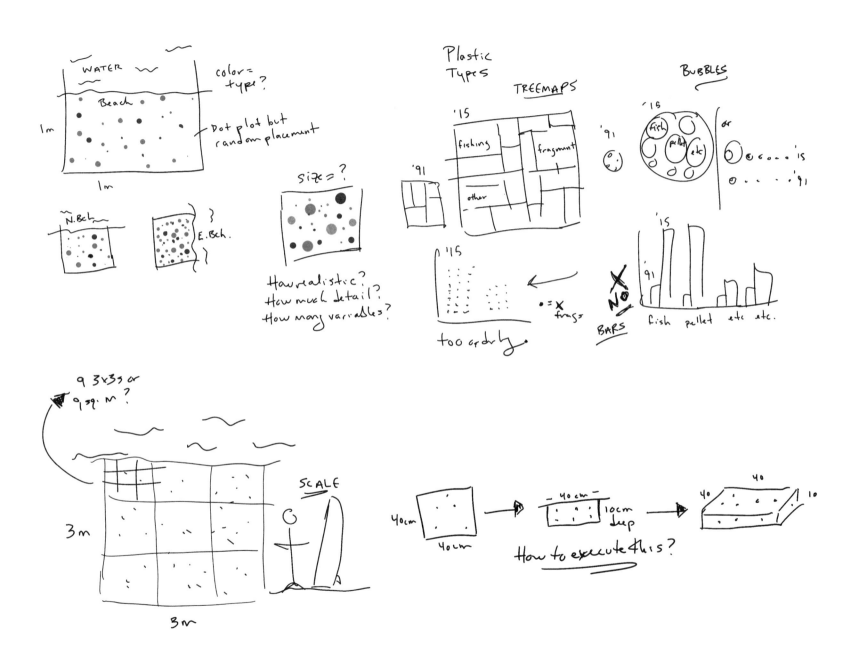

WATER

color = type?

Beach

1m

Dot plot but random placement

1m

N.Bch.

E.Bch.

size = ?

How realistic?
How much detail?
How many variables?

Plastic Types

TREEMAPS

'15

fishing

fragment

other

'91

'91

'15

BUBBLES

'15

fish

pellet

etc

or

'15

'91

'15

• = x frags

too orderly

NO

BARS

'91

fish pellet etc etc.

9 3x3s or
9 sq. m?

SCALE

3m

3m

40cm

40cm

40 cm

10cm deep

40

40

10

How to execute this?

thinking about before-and-after construction, using the same form twice: once for 1991 and once for 2015, to show the dramatic change.

Here I found myself pausing naturally. I was focused on the treemap and thinking of ways to make it work. That signaled it was time to prototype.

Prototype

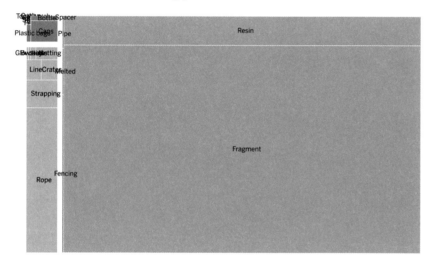

A prototype of the treemap made using an online tool called Raw helped me realize that the form would be difficult to work with. It might seem that the labels assigned to such small values are what make this hard to use, and they're part of it. But the

bigger part for me was the overwhelming size of the fragment and resin blocks. They dominated so fully that I feared people wouldn't even see the other categories, losing the sense that the other plastic is also accumulating at high volumes. And I recognized that this is the 2015 data. If I made the 1991 data to scale, the map would be about one-tenth the size, and the categories of plastic with smaller amounts would virtually disappear.

I suspected that bubbles within bubbles would suffer the same fate, so I did a quick paper prototype of the individual bubbles I had sketched as a hedge and hit on what I decided to use. Because these are prototypes, I used approximations of actual data to get a sense of how the visual would fall on a page or a screen. It doesn't take much to see my thinking progress here. I prototyped two categories of plastic and decided that I'd be visualizing too many individual items, many of which would be proportionally tiny. So I decided to go back to the data and regroup it. I created five categories and started to think about color contrast for the two years. This seemed more manageable for an audience to take in. As I was doing this, I also thought I'd have an opportunity to show just one simple total for each year. I was thinking ahead to the presentation—being able to show the 1991 dot and then dramatically revealing the 2015 dot.

I also needed to prototype the beach scenes. Again, I approximated real data, randomly distributing the right number of dots. The effect was exactly what

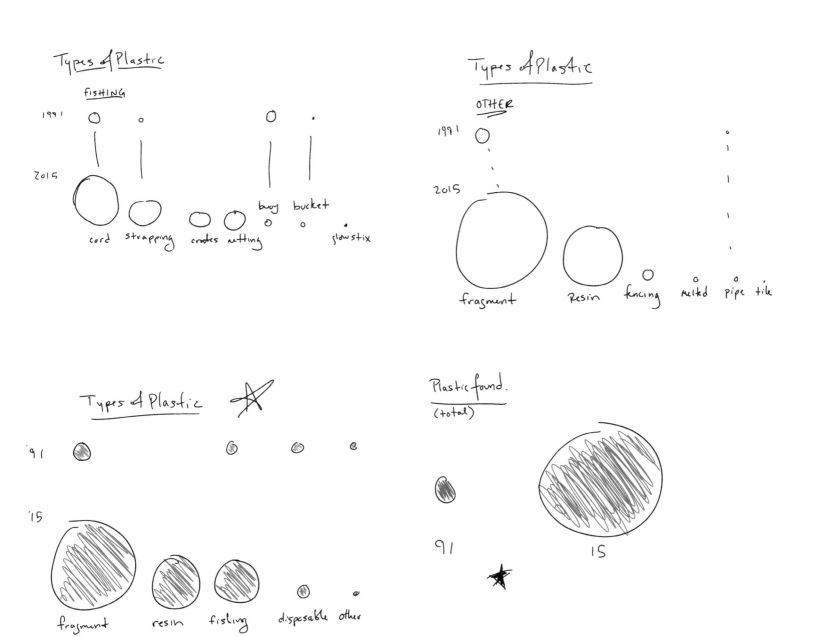

I was hoping for. This left me with some concerns about showing East Beach, where the numbers were an order of magnitude higher, but I figured I could tackle that as I developed the actual visual—a process I still had to figure out.

All told, I spent about an hour prototyping. What you don't see here are a couple of starts and stops and crossings out. Prototyping is iterative, but all the iterations are on the same idea, whereas with sketching, you're generating many new ideas.

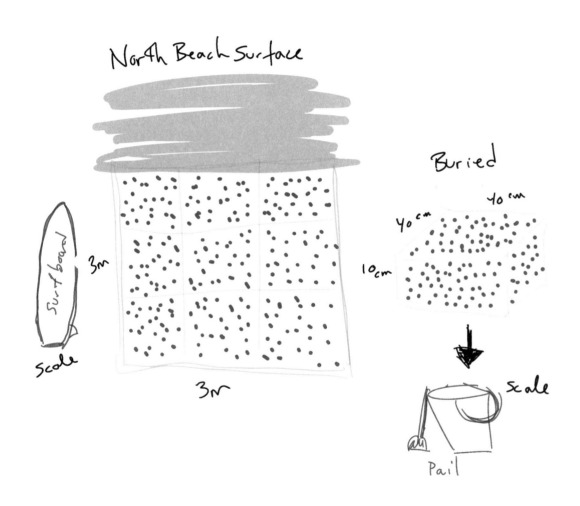

Final Charts and Presentation

This presentation took about four hours to construct using Adobe Illustrator. I found tools in Illustrator to create the random spread of dots and to count them (the data is accurate within a few dots, plus or minus) and to create three-dimensional cuts of sand. My concerns about the density of East Beach data were warranted, but using some transparency in the dots helped to make that density a virtue rather than a problem: you get the sense in these charts of plastic literally piling up.

I understand if that time investment seems excessive at first. But consider what you're trying to accomplish in the most important presentations you give: To create change? To get buy-in or money? To start a movement or alter behavior? At times like that, investing a few hours in a beyond-standard presentation that makes ideas pop off the page is reasonable. A professional designer could probably have created this more quickly than I did (and when your presentation is crucial, that's a worthy investment).

As lengthy as this may look, it can be presented in under five minutes. The number of slides matters far less than the time to comprehension for each slide. Stuffing too many ideas into one slide will have your audience trying to read through what you're showing, independent of what you're saying. It risks their focusing on the wrong thing or making the wrong interpretation. Here I don't

1

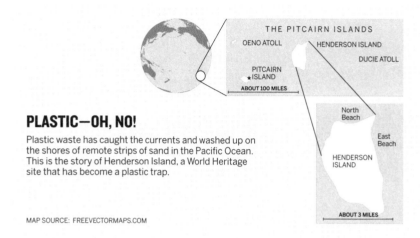

PLASTIC—OH, NO!

Plastic waste has caught the currents and washed up on the shores of remote strips of sand in the Pacific Ocean. This is the story of Henderson Island, a World Heritage site that has become a plastic trap.

MAP SOURCE: FREEVECTORMAPS.COM

2

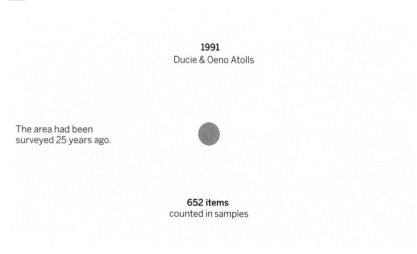

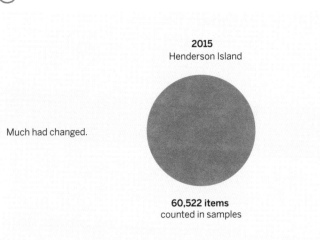

2015
Henderson Island

Much had changed.

60,522 items
counted in samples

4

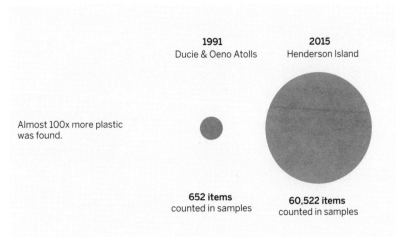

1991
Ducie & Oeno Atolls

2015
Henderson Island

Almost 100x more plastic
was found.

652 items
counted in samples

60,522 items
counted in samples

give an audience more than one or two ideas per slide to think about. Imagine, for example, the first six slides all in one. That's a lot of information to take in—where in the world we are, what the totals are, how the totals break down—and I'd probably need to spend a few minutes or more on that. Additionally, the visuals would have to be smaller, and the sheer volume of visual information would make it hard to know how to proceed through the slide. By breaking it down, I can allow mere seconds for each slide, because comprehension is nearly instant. Furthermore, breaking up the visualizations creates plenty of drama in this presentation. A skilled presenter will exploit this by, for example, pausing after showing the 1991 data before revealing the 2015 data.

Despite the amount of information I've included, there are really only two ideas here: a comparison of past to present, and the present state in two places. For the second, notice that I use setup visualizations without data. This is another canny technique for presentations. It trains the audience on a chart's structure before they use it. By the time the data is added, they already understand what field we're playing on. Again, I'm controlling the experience, taking the audience with me rather than showing them everything and hoping they can follow.

The surfboard and the pail are not trivial clip art additions to support the idea that we're on a beach. They're there for scale. Showing nine square meters without some point of reference would make it harder to relate the visualization space to the real world. The same is true for the pail and the buried plastic. You may notice that I adjusted the size of the cross-section of sand from 40 cm × 40 cm × 10 cm to 1 m × 1 m × 10 cm. That meant more calculations for me, but I thought that by matching the size to one of the surface sections in the 3 m × 3 m diagrams, I would help people understand better. Now they can look at those buried samples and imagine each fitting into one of those square-meter sections.

Some minor notes: The introductory slide sets us in space: You Are Here. Notice that the captions on each slide are very short. I don't want people reading the slide. Also notice that they don't explicitly repeat what the visual shows but they do add to understanding. Instead of reporting the amount of debris on North and East Beaches, which you can see, the caption frames what you're looking at by noting that East Beach is eight times as bad as North Beach. The last slide is included to show that it's easy to create a summary of the story for a presentation handout. Rather than trying to visualize the massive estimation numbers, I used type as a visual element.

Finally, a word about precision. It's clear that my approach values a *sense* of the data over its precise numbers. I grouped elements so that I wouldn't be dealing with too many variables with the types of plastic. I used a random distribution technique in which individual data values crashed into and piled on top of one another—which, one might argue, masks some of the values. I used very few

5

1991
Ducie & Oeno Atolls

● Fragments

In 1991 the surveys found 13 types of plastic in four categories.

● Fishing
● Disposable items
• Other

6

1991
Ducie & Oeno Atolls

2015
Henderson Island

Fragments

2015: 24 types of plastic in five categories.

Resin

Fishing

Disposable items
Other

7

Researchers surveyed surface debris on two beaches, North Beach and East Beach. They literally **counted plastic things**.

3 m

3 m

8

North Beach

● 1 plastic item (dots not to scale)

North Beach was heavily polluted with plastic.

270 items
per 9 square meters

specific numbers in the presentation. To me, for this challenge and the context I was working in—help a lay audience *feel* what's happening on Henderson Island with plastic—this trade-off was OK. I thought the idea of a gigantic difference between the past and the present, and the idea of saturation in the present data, was more valuable than the specific values.

That's not always a good approach. In many cases it just won't work. The chart will come off as obfuscatory or overdesigned. Even in this case I can imagine academics and data scientists blanching. This isn't data visualization, they might say, but a design exercise.

I'll defend it as data visualization, albeit heavy on the design. I used real values and proportions. I tried to remain true to the data that was reported and the spirit of what's being communicated: massive volumes of plastic are washing up on the shores of Henderson Island. If someone wanted the specific data, I would provide it, of course. Even so, I imagine that many more-traditional charted interpretations of this data could be as effective or more effective. I look forward to seeing some.

9

East Beach

● 1 plastic item
(dots not
to scale)

East Beach was **8 times as bad**.

2,151 items
per 9 square meters

10

Researchers also dug down to find smaller pieces
of plastic that had been buried over time.

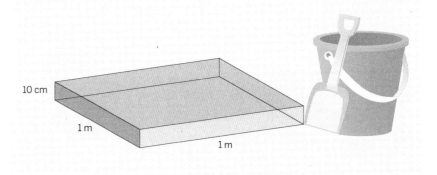

10 cm

1 m

1 m

11

Plastic debris had seeped into the sand on North Beach.

North Beach

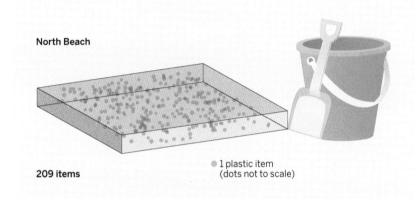

209 items

● 1 plastic item
(dots not to scale)

12

East Beach sand teemed with plastic.

East Beach

2,573 items

● 1 plastic item
(dots not to scale)

13

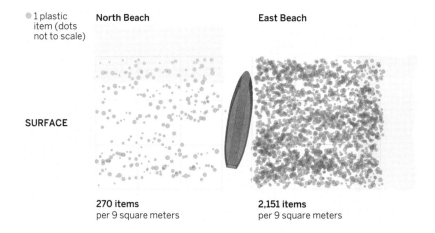

● 1 plastic item (dots not to scale)

North Beach

East Beach

SURFACE

270 items
per 9 square meters

2,151 items
per 9 square meters

14

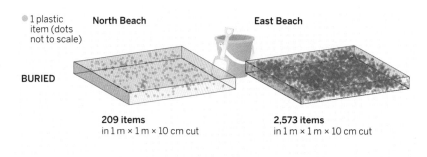

● 1 plastic item (dots not to scale)

North Beach

East Beach

BURIED

209 items
in 1 m × 1 m × 10 cm cut

2,573 items
in 1 m × 1 m × 10 cm cut

ESTIMATED TOTALS FOR HENDERSON ISLAND

37,800,000 PIECES OF PLASTIC, WEIGHING...

16,797 KILOGRAMS

GLOSSARY OF CHART TYPES

2 × 2 matrix: Box bisected horizontally and vertically to create four quadrants. Often used to illustrate a typology based on two variables. (Also called a *matrix*.)

+ Easy-to-use organizing principle for categorizing elements and creating "zones"

– Plotting items within quadrants at different spatial intervals suggests a statistical relationship that likely doesn't exist

Alluvial diagram: Nodes and streams show how values move from one point to another. Often used to show changes over time or details in how values are organized, such as how budget allocations are spent month by month. (Also called a *flow diagram*.)

+ Exposes detail in value changes or exposes detailed breakdowns in broad categories of data

– Many values and changes in flow make for complex, crisscrossed visuals that, while pretty, may be difficult to interpret

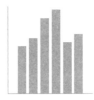

Bar chart: Height or length of bars shows relationship between categories ("categorical data"). Often used to compare discrete groups on the same measure, such as salaries of ten different CEOs. (Also called a *column chart* when bars are vertical.)

+ Familiar form that's universally understood; great for simple comparisons between categories

– Many bars may create the impression of a trend line rather than highlight discrete values; multiple groups of bars may become difficult to parse

Bubble chart: Dots scattered along two measures that add a third (size of bubble) and sometimes fourth (color of bubble) dimension to the data to show distributions of several variables. Often used to show complex relationships, such as multiple pieces of demographic data plotted by country. (Also called, erroneously, a *scatter plot*.)

+ One of the simplest ways to incorporate a "z-axis"; bubble sizes can add crucial context to distribution visuals

– Sizing bubbles proportionally is tricky (area is not proportional to radius); by their nature, three- and four-axis charts require more time to parse, so are less ideal for at-a-glance presentation

Bump chart: Lines show change in ordinal rank over time. Often used to show popularity, such as box office rankings week to week. (Also called a *bumps chart*.)

+ Simple way to express popularity, winners, and losers

− Changes aren't statistically significant (values are ordinal, not cardinal); many levels and more change make for eye-catching skeins but may make it difficult to follow rankings

Flow chart: Polygons and arrows arranged to show a process or workflow. Often used to map out decision making, how data moves through a system, or how people interact with systems, such as the process a user goes through to buy a product on a website. (Also called a *decision tree*, which is one type of flow chart.)

+ Formalized system, universally accepted, for representing a process with many decision points

− Must understand established syntax (e.g., diamonds represent decision points; parallelograms represent input/output, etc.)

Dot plot: Shows several measures along a single axis. Often used in place of a bar chart when the comparison that matters is not the height of each bar but the difference in height between bars.

+ Compact form that works vertically or horizontally in a small space; makes comparison much easier than the traditional form (bar chart) along a single measure

− With many dots to plot, can be difficult to label effectively; removes any sense of trend across categories if that's important

Geographical chart: Maps used to represent values attributed to locations in the physical world. Often used to compare values between countries or regions, such as a map showing political affiliations. (Also called a *map*.)

+ Familiarity with geography makes it easy to find values and compare them at multiple levels (i.e., comparing data by country and region simultaneously)

− Using the size of places to represent other values can over- or underrepresent the value encoded in those places

Hierarchical chart: Lines and points used to show the relationship and relative rank of a collection of elements. Often used to show how an organization is structured, such as a family or a company. (Also called an *org chart,* a *family tree,* or a *tree chart,* all of which are types of hierarchies.)

+ Easily understood method for documenting and illustrating relationships and complex structures

− Line-and-box approach limited in the amount of complexity it can show; harder to show less formal relationships such as how people work together outside the bounds of a corporate hierarchy

Histogram: Bars show distribution based on the frequency of occurrences for each value in a range. Often used to show probability, such as the results of a risk-analysis simulation. (Also called, erroneously, a *bar chart,* which compares values between categories, whereas a histogram shows the distribution of values for one variable.)

+ A fundamental chart type used to show statistical distribution and probability

− Audiences sometimes mistake a histogram for a bar chart

Line chart: Connected points show how values change, usually over time (continuous data). Often used to compare trends by plotting multiple lines together, such as revenues for several companies. (Also called a *fever chart* or a *trend line.*)

+ Familiar form that's universally understood; great for at-a-glance representation of trends

− Focusing on the trend line makes it harder to see and talk about discrete data points; too many trend lines make it difficult to see any individual line

Lollipop chart: Similar to a dot plot, but plots two points on a single measure connected by a line to show some relationship between the two values. Plotting several lollipops can create an effect similar to a floating bar chart, in which values aren't all anchored to the same point. (Also called a *double lollipop chart.*)

+ Compact form that works horizontally and vertically; great for making multiple comparisons between two variables when the difference between the two is what matters most

− When variables "flip" (the high value was the low value in a previous lollipop), it can be confusing to read across multiple lollipops; multiple lollipops of similar value make it hard to evaluate individual items in the chart

Metaphorical chart: Arrows, pyramids, circles, and other well-recognized figures used to show a nonstatistical concept. Often used to represent abstract ideas and processes, such as business cycles.

+ Can simplify complex ideas; universal recognition of metaphors makes understanding feel innate

– Easy to mix metaphors, misapply them, or overdesign them

Network diagram: Nodes and lines connected to show the relationship between elements within a group. Often used to show interconnectedness of physical things, such as computers or people.

+ Helps illustrate relationships between nodes that might otherwise be hard to see; highlights clusters and outliers

– Networks tend to get complex quickly. Some network diagrams, while beautiful, can become difficult to interpret

Pie chart: A circle divided into sections that each represent some variable's proportion of the whole value. Often used to show simple breakdowns of totals, such as population demographics. (Also called a *donut chart*, a variation shown as a ring.)

+ Ubiquitous chart type; shows dominant versus nondominant shares well

– People don't estimate the area of pie wedges very well; more than a few slices makes values hard to distinguish and quantify

Sankey diagram: Arrows or bars show how values are distributed and transferred. Often used to show the flow of physical quantities, such as energy or people. (Also called a *flow diagram*.)

+ Exposes detail in system flows; helps identify dominant components and inefficiencies

– Complex systems with many components and flow paths make for complex diagrams

Scatter plot: Dots plotted against two variables show the relationship between those two variables for a particular set of data. Often used to detect and show correlation, such as a plot of people's ages against their incomes. (Also called a *scatter diagram*, *scatter chart*, or *scatter*.)

+ A basic chart type that most people are familiar with; spatial approach makes it easy to see correlation, negative correlation, clusters, and outliers

– Shows correlation so well that people may make a causal leap even though correlation doesn't imply causation

Slope chart: Lines show a simple change in values. Often used to show dramatic change or outliers that run counter to most of the slopes, such as revenues falling in one region while rising in all others. (Also called a *line chart*.)

+ Creates a simple before-and-after narrative that's easy to see and grasp either for individual values or as an aggregate trend for many values

– Excludes all detail of what happened to the values between the two states; too many crisscrossing lines may make it hard to see changes in individual values

Small multiples: A series of small charts, usually line charts, that show different categories measured on the same scale. Often used to show simple trends dozens of times over, such as GDP trends by country. (Also called *grid charts* or *trellis charts*.)

+ Makes simple comparisons across multiple, even dozens, of categories more accessible than if all the lines were stacked in one chart

– Without dramatic change or difference, can be hard to find meaning in the comparison; some "events" you'd see in a single chart, such as crossover points between variables, are lost

Stacked area chart: Lines plot a particular variable over time, and the area between lines is filled with color to emphasize volume or cumulative totals. Often used to show multiple values proportionally over time, such as product sales volume for several products over the course of a year. (Also called an *area chart*.)

+ Shows changing proportions over time well; empha-sizes a sense of volume or accumulation

– Too many "layers" create slices so thin it's hard to see changes or differences or track values over time

Stacked bar chart: Rectangles divided into sections that each represent some variable's proportion to the whole. Often used to show simple breakdowns of totals, such as sales by region. (Also called a *proportional bar chart*.)

+ Some consider it a superior alternative to a pie chart; shows dominant versus nondominant shares well; may effectively handle more categories than a pie chart; works horizontally and vertically

– Including too many categories or grouping multiple stacked bars together may make it difficult to see differences and changes

Table: Information arranged in columns and rows. Often used to show individual values over time across multiple categories, such as quarterly financial performance.

+ Makes every individual value available; easier to read and compare values than a prose version of the same information

– Difficult to get an at-a-glance sense of trends or to make quick comparisons between groups of values

Treemap: A rectangle divided into smaller rectangles that each represent some variable's proportion to the whole value. Often used to show hierarchical proportions, such as a budget divided into categories and subcategories.

+ Compact form for showing detailed proportional breakdowns; overcomes some limitations of pie charts with many slices

– Detail-oriented form not optimal for at-a-glance understanding; too many categories makes for a stunning but harder-to-parse visual; usually requires software capable of accurately arranging the squares.

Unit chart: Dots or icons arranged to represent collections of individual values associated with categorical variables. Often used to show tallies of physical items, such as dollars spent or people stricken in an epidemic. (Also called a *dot chart* or *dot plot*.)

+ Represents values in a way that feels more concrete, less abstract than some statistical representations

– Too many unit categories may make it hard to focus on central meaning; strong design skills needed to make arrangement of units most effective

CHART TYPE GUIDE

THIS GUIDE, CREATED by Andrew Abela, is a good starting point for thinking about chart types, but try not to use it as a decision engine. Not everyone will agree with his organization of the types, and the hierarchy doesn't include every effective chart type. Indeed, each chart shown here has numerous variations and hybrids, and new ones are being created all the time. Plus this tool may narrow your thinking at a stage when you want to be expansive and experiment with multiple approaches. But it will help you understand categories of forms—comparison versus distribution, for example—and it may inspire you to try something. I've adapted it to work with the talk-sketch-prototype framework laid out here in chapter 6 and in the original *Good Charts*. See the following page for that adaptation.

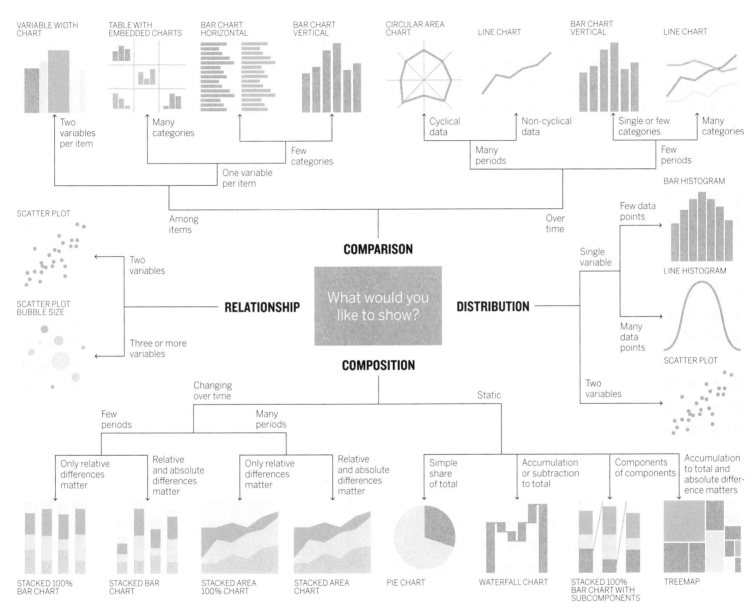

VARIABLE WIDTH CHART

TABLE WITH EMBEDDED CHARTS

BAR CHART HORIZONTAL

BAR CHART VERTICAL

CIRCULAR AREA CHART

LINE CHART

BAR CHART VERTICAL

LINE CHART

Two variables per item

Many categories

One variable per item

Few categories

Cyclical data

Non-cyclical data

Many periods

Single or few categories

Many categories

Few periods

BAR HISTOGRAM

Among items

Over time

Few data points

SCATTER PLOT

Single variable

LINE HISTOGRAM

Two variables

COMPARISON

What would you like to show?

RELATIONSHIP

DISTRIBUTION

SCATTER PLOT BUBBLE SIZE

Three or more variables

Many data points

SCATTER PLOT

COMPOSITION

Two variables

Changing over time

Static

Few periods

Many periods

Only relative differences matter

Relative and absolute differences matter

Only relative differences matter

Relative and absolute differences matter

Simple share of total

Accumulation or subtraction to total

Components of components

Accumulation to total and absolute difference matters

STACKED 100% BAR CHART

STACKED BAR CHART

STACKED AREA 100% CHART

STACKED AREA CHART

PIE CHART

WATERFALL CHART

STACKED 100% BAR CHART WITH SUBCOMPONENTS

TREEMAP

SOURCE: ANDREW V. ABELA

APPENDIX C

KEYWORDS FOR CHART TYPES

COMPARISONS

NOTES

before/after
categories
compare
contrast
over time
peaks
rank
trend
types
valleys

BARS	BUMP	LINES	SLOPE	SMALL MULTIPLES

DISTRIBUTIONS

NOTES

alluvial
cluster
distributed
from/to
plotted
points
spread
spread over
relative to
transfer

ALLUVIALS	BUBBLE	HISTOGRAM	SANKEY	SCATTER

COMPOSITIONS

NOTES

components   slices
divvied up   subsections
group   total
makes up
of the whole
parts
percentage
pieces
portion
proportion

PIE	STACKED AREA	STACKED BAR	TREEMAP	UNIT

MAPS
NETWORKS
LOGIC

NOTES

cluster   places
complex   relationships
connections   routes
group   structure
hierarchy   space
if/then   yes/no
network
organize
paths

FLOW CHART	GEOGRAPHY	HIERARCHIES	2 X 2	NETWORKS

ACKNOWLEDGMENTS

Throughout this workbook I use the metaphor of learning to play the guitar to describe how to learn to make good charts. Making a good book is different than that; it's more like staging an arena rock show. In the end we see the band and hear its songs, but really we're witnessing the skilled work of a legion of professionals. Without them, the band would fail; the experience would stink. Same goes for a picture book like this one, a beast that requires more than ordinary bookcraft.

Fortunate as I am, I'm surrounded by the most extraordinary craftspeople. It starts with my editor and friend, **Jeff Kehoe**, whose keen eye and instincts for what readers need is unparalleled. I also count myself lucky to have the most supportive leadership at Harvard Business Publishing, especially **Adi Ignatius** and **Amy Bernstein**, who afford me the great luxury of this second life as an author. Though he has moved on, I'm indebted, too, to friend and former colleague **Tim Sullivan** for giving me a chance in the first place and always believing in my vision for *Good Charts*.

A book with nearly 300 images in it puts plenty of pressure on the production staff of Harvard Business Review Press, but you'd never know it from their calm exteriors and graceful execution. Special thanks to **Jennifer Waring**, for managing it all beautifully without betraying any panic though I'm sure I caused plenty, and to **Allison Peter** for keeping me (mostly) on track. Thanks also to **Greg Mroczek** for finding the right paper and managing the printing of this beautiful book, and to **Ralph Fowler** for expert typesetting of a complex manuscript.

I've been stewarded the past two years by a great marketing team who are as much a part of the success of *Good Charts* as anyone. Thank you, **Julie Devoll**, **Lindsey Dietrich**, **Nina Nocciolino** (we miss you), and **Kenzie Travers**.

The countless attendees at my lectures and workshops on data visualization often inspired me and challenged me, and many of their ideas are reflected in this workbook. When I speak on data visualization, I'm often approached by someone who wants to know about the colors I use, or the typography; or they ask how I design my charts. Many admire the artistic style of *Good Charts* itself. I take no credit for any of this. Credit goes first and foremost to my dear friend and creative nonpareil **James de Vries**, a designer and force of nature whose influence is still felt on this side of the world, even though he's moved back to the other side. I'm also deeply indebted to **Stephani Finks** for refining designs for this workbook and its cover, and for inspiring me. I can't speak of design without also celebrating the contributions of my friend, colleague, and collaborator **Marta Kusztra**, who taught me to love gray, be bold, show less, and fight banality.

Thank you to **Martha Spaulding**, a gifted editor with an uncanny ability to create efficient grace from sloppy prose. And thank you to **Matthew Perry**, a fellow admirer of good information design, who took my amateurish work in Illustrator and turned it into professional-grade charting. Thank you to HBR for allowing me to show, alter, and sometimes undo, charts published by HBR in the past.

Many of the challenges created for this workbook came from colleagues. I am indebted to them for allowing me to use derivations of their real-world dataviz work in various forms here, and for advising me, working with me, and trusting me to develop them into challenges. They include: **Alison Beard**, **Walter Frick**, **Gretchen Gavett**, **Sarah Green Carmichael**, **Maureen Hoch**, **Tyler Machado**, **Dan McGinn**, **Gardiner Morse**, **Emily Neville-O'Neill**, and **Marianne Weichselbaum**. Special thanks to my neighbors at HBR, **Ania Wieckowski** and **Dave Lievens**, who never missed an opportunity to send me down some dataviz rabbit hole by suggesting I fix this chart or that, or even just wondering aloud how many days a year the high temperature is in the 70s. And thank you to the active members of the dataviz Slack channel at HBR, a constant source of inspiration, learning, and amusement.

A special thank you to **Sally Ashworth**, my London colleague and friend, for taking care of me and for the endless support. And to **Susan Francis**, for always supporting, constantly listening, and never sugarcoating.

If I've forgotten you, I apologize, and I will buy you a drink.

We are the product of our upbringing, and I had a good one thanks to my family, especially my parents, **Vin** and **Paula**, and my siblings and their partners, **Lisa** and **John**, **Michael** and **Courtney**, **Matthew** and **David**, and **Mark** and **Amy**.

As ever, thank you to **Sara**, **Emily**, **Molly**, and **Piper** for lingering here awhile in the foolishness of things.

ABOUT THE AUTHOR

Scott Berinato, self-professed dataviz geek, is the author of *Good Charts: The HBR Guide to Making Smarter, More Persuasive Data Visualizations*, of which *Fast Company* said, "It may just be the design manual of the year." Presentation guru Nancy Duarte called *Good Charts* "the book I wish I'd written." Berinato speaks frequently on the power and necessity of good data visualization—his most recent talk being his third consecutive year presenting on dataviz at SXSW in Austin, Texas—and has worked with many companies and individuals to up their dataviz game. He is a senior editor at *Harvard Business Review*, where he writes and edits articles about visualization as well as technology and business.